SOUS·VIDE

Made Simple

SOUS·VIDE
Made Simple

LISA Q. FETTERMAN, MEESHA HALM, and SCOTT PEABODY
Photography by MONICA LO

TEN SPEED PRESS
California | New York

CONTENTS

INTRODUCTION

"What's for dinner?" These seemingly innocent words can strike dread in the heart of anyone managing a busy household. If you know me (or have read my first book), you know how much I love cooking. But after a long day at the office, juggling errands and kids, the prospect of getting even a simple dinner on the table can feel like climbing Everest. The last thing I want is for cooking to feel like yet another chore on my to-do list.

When my husband and I launched Nomiku as the first sous vide company geared toward home cooks, I managed to find the energy to make elaborate meals in between long hours at the office. But that, as my coauthor and friend Meesha is wont to say, was BC—Before Children. Five years later, my passion for cooking delicious meals at home hasn't slowed down, but neither has life. As my company continues to grow, so do the two mini people I created—my wonderful son and daughter, Zech and Mari. Crazy busy has become my norm.

Then I had a revelation. While I was crisscrossing the country evangelizing sous vide as the perfect tool for making exceptional restaurant-quality meals at home, it dawned on me that it could solve the unglamorous but more pressing challenge of getting food on the table every night.

Despite its rapidly expanding popularity, sous vide—the technique of cooking sealed food in a precise temperature water bath—is still widely misunderstood as something meant only for top chefs and other culinary obsessives. Even among those who already own home immersion circulators—1 million converts and counting—it still tends to be reserved for special occasions or ambitious projects. I want to change all that! That's why I launched Nomiku Meals, a frozen-food meal delivery service that brings ready-to-reheat sous vide meals to your door. But for those of us who want both convenience and the satisfaction of cooking a homemade meal, this book teaches you how to prepare your own delicious sous vide weeknight meals with ease.

In contrast to my first book, *Sous Vide at Home*, which showed ambitious home cooks how to re-create elaborate dishes like duck confit and butter-poached lobster, this book is aimed at home cooks (sous vide novices and old hands alike) who simply want to make delicious everyday meals with readily available ingredients and with minimal effort. The key is preparing everyday standbys like chicken or salmon in advance, to be used as the building blocks for an endless variety of delicious, unfussy meals on short notice. I want you to be able to come home from work, open up your fridge, and quickly whip up a tasty, nutritious dinner—which is why you won't find me calling for exotic ingredients that will take up more of your precious time to hunt down. The recipes in this book require only common ingredients that you either already have in your pantry or can easily pick up at a local Mexican bodega, Asian market, or in the international aisle of a grocery store. And anything you can't sleuth out on foot can be ordered online and shipped to your door. Whether you're craving cheesy chicken parm, juicy grilled pork chops, or Korean barbecue–style beef, the recipes in this book are impressive enough to serve to guests, yet quick and simple enough to make for your family on a Monday night.

HOW TO USE THIS BOOK

This book is organized into chapters centered around fourteen "master recipes," simple instructions designed to teach you how to use sous vide to prepare the workhorses of everyday cooking with sensational results. Each master recipe is followed by three "spin-off" recipes that transform the master into a finished dish. I did my best to showcase a variety of cooking techniques and cuisines, and also provided additional serving suggestions, so you'll never get bored. Like buying precut vegetables or marinated meats, preparing these foundational ingredients in advance offers both convenience and versatility. The tender chicken thighs cooked on Sunday night can be made into hearty chicken pot pies or a zingy low-carb chicken stir-fry with red pepper and pineapple later in the week. Likewise, succulent, slow-cooked braised beef can become richly spiced Thai curry or a beef Bourguignon par excellence in next to no time.

This do-ahead approach also gives you the freedom to stock your fridge for the week without committing yourself to any particular dish. Just cook and store the master recipe for chicken breasts or pork loin over the weekend, and then on Wednesday decide at dinnertime whether you want to make pasta, salad, or stir-fry with them, depending on your mood and what other ingredients you have on hand.

In this book you'll also find a handful of stand-alone bonus recipes, such as the Deluxe Stuffed Cheeseburger (page 98), that I simply didn't want you to miss. And while everyone knows that sous vide does a miraculous job of cooking meats, to show just how versatile this cooking method can be, I've also included recipes for vegetable side dishes, fork-and-knife salads, and plant-based mains that are substantial enough to play a starring role. And the icing on the cake? I spell out how sous vide can help you add swag to your dessert game by mastering just one simple custard base recipe!

For each master recipe, I've provided a range of time, from the minimum to the outermost time required to yield the best results. I've also indicated the time required to prepare the final spin-off dishes, assuming the main ingredient has already been cooked. Nearly all of them can be prepped and finished using a conventional cooking method, and on the table in under an hour (most of them take fewer than 30 minutes). You certainly can make the spin-off dishes in one go; just factor in the additional time it takes to sous vide the master recipe.

Before jumping into the recipes, I encourage you to read the following sections on how sous vide works, tips on storage and reheating, and critical information on food safety. I also recommend you read the master recipes all the way through before you begin cooking the spin-offs. Approach each section of the book as a mini masterclass on sous vide cooking—try preparing several, if not all, of the master recipes and their corresponding spin-off dishes a few times until they become second nature.

And should you ever tire of my collection of lovingly selected recipes and variations (inconceivable!), I'm still confident that you will get a lifetime of use out of this book. Once you get the hang of it, you'll be ready to experiment on your own to create an endless variety of dishes by adapting your own recipes to use this approach (see page 180 for tips on how to do this).

GETTING STARTED

If you're new to sous vide cooking, you may be asking yourself "what's all the hype about?" Allow me to explain.

WHAT'S SOUS VIDE GOT TO DO WITH IT?

Although *sous vide* (SOO VEED) is French for "under vacuum" (referring to the fact that food is cooked in sealed bags), what truly sets the technique apart is precise temperature control. This precision means you can achieve consistently perfect cooking, regardless of skill level, with no need to stand watch over a hot pan, since your food's internal temperature will never rise above that of the surrounding water and overcook. Sous vide also provides ample buffer time in which you can hold food at a steady temperature—hours, in most cases—without compromising the quality. In short, sous vide offers all the convenience of a slow cooker or crock pot, but with drastically better, reliably excellent results.

FROM HOSPITALS TO HOME COOKING

Although sous vide began as a method for industrial food production in places such as hospitals and large-scale commercial manufacturers, where it was valued for improving efficiency, safety, and storability, it found its wings after being introduced into the world of French fine dining in the late 1970s. For decades, sous vide has been the secret weapon of Michelin-starred chefs who value its uncanny ability to produce exact results, and employ it in their kitchens to make flavorful, ethereally textured food: succulent meats, delicate seafood, toothsome vegetables. Part of the reason that sous vide remained the exclusive domain of fancy restaurants for so long was cost: only a short while ago, these machines cost thousands of dollars—definitely out of reach for the average home cook. But thanks to the introduction of affordable (under $200) circulators, often referred to as sous vide machines, this cooking method is more accessible now than ever.

It's also dead simple.

EASY AS 1, 2, 3: SEASONING, COOKING, AND FINISHING

The key tool for cooking sous vide is a thermal immersion circulator, a device that clamps onto the side of a pot or other heatproof vessel, and heats and circulates water to reach and maintain an exact temperature. To do this at home, fill a pot with water, set the circulator to the desired temperature, and let the water heat up. Then simply season your food, seal it in an airtight, food-safe plastic bag (see Sealing, page 12), drop the bag into the bath when it reaches the target temperature, and then wait for the length of time specified in the recipe. Once your food is cooked, you can cool and store it for another time, or transform it into a final dish right away with a choice of finishing techniques (grilling, frying, roasting) to build additional flavor and texture. These three basic steps—seasoning, cooking, and finishing—are the heart of sous vide cooking.

STEP 1: SEASON JUDICIOUSLY BEFORE YOU BAG

If you follow sous vide cooking, you've almost certainly seen handsome images of sealed bags of beautifully seared meats with winsome sprigs of herbs and a tantalizing knob of butter. But in almost every master recipe in this book, I call for nothing but salt in the bag—no herbs, no spices, no fats (though in the case of fish I do use a small amount of oil to prevent sticking).

Why is that? The truth is, salt is the only seasoning that actually penetrates beyond the surface of most foods (see A Note on Salt, page 25); all those other ingredients do very little to infuse flavor into your food. While it's true that meals would be terribly monotonous with salt as their only flavoring, dry rubs and marinades are really only a surface seasoning—and much of that seasoning will end up in the liquid released as the food cooks, rather than on the food itself. The same is true of fats like butter, which will absorb flavor in the bag but do very little to impart it. Aromatic ingredients are another item I recommend

1.

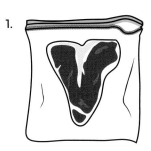

2.

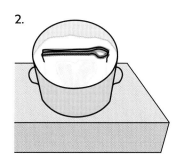

3.

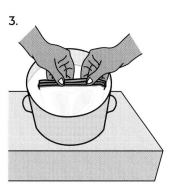

4.

skipping. Aside from being inefficient, many—especially raw garlic and fresh herbs—become overpowering or harsh when cooked sous vide due to the relatively low temperatures, long cooking times, and lack of evaporation.

There's another advantage to cooking foods with this less-is-more-approach: leaving your main ingredient au naturel allows you to transform it in any number of ways, making it a versatile base for future recipes. (It also makes it easy to accommodate even the pickiest of eaters—plain grilled chicken breast for one, coming up!)

Despite the above caveats, I certainly don't condemn preseasoning sous vide food in every circumstance. In fact, there are specific situations where it makes a lot of sense to add aromatics to your bag, such as when preparing vegetables, custards, and one-bag meals. I'll explain these exceptions when we get to them.

STEP 2: SEALING, COOKING, AND DONENESS

Although *sous vide* literally means "under vacuum," you don't need a vacuum sealing machine to cook sous vide. Following are the basics for getting it done right.

SEALING

The sole purpose of sealing food in plastic bags is to prevent evaporation and the leaching of flavors and nutrients into the surrounding air or water. All you really need is a food-grade, heat-safe plastic bag—any freezer bag with an airtight seal will do (see Essential Equipment, page 20)—and to follow a few easy steps for sealing it using one of two methods.

Water displacement method
To get most of the air out of a bag and achieve a proper seal without using an expensive vacuum sealer, I recommend the water displacement method (aka Archimedes's principle). (1) Place the food, including any marinade or sauce, in a freezer-safe, double-sealed ziplock bag. (2) Submerge the open bag into the water with only the seal exposed. Everything below the zippered closing should be covered with water. The barometric pressure of the water will force most of the air out of the bag. (3) When the liquid rises to just below the zipper, seal the bag. You should feel and hear the "click-click-click" as it closes. When placing a lot of small items in a bag, strive to arrange all of the pieces in a single layer, without overlapping. This ensures that the pieces will cook through evenly. (4) Once the bag is sealed, run your hand over the pouch again to distribute the contents uniformly before placing the bag in the water bath.

Table-edge method

Sealing bags that contain liquid, such as soups, custards, alcohol infusions, and one-bag meals (see page 177), can be awkward and messy. Here is a hassle-free solution that I call the table-edge method. (1) Pour the ingredients into a freezer-safe, double-sealed ziplock bag and partially close the seal. (2) Hold the bag against a table (or counter) with the liquid hanging down and the top of the bag (with the zippered closing) on top of the table. (3) Use the edge of the table to push down on the liquid, and then (4) push out any remaining air from the top of the bag before sealing it closed.

COOKING

Once your food is properly sealed in the bag, it's simply a matter of submerging it into a preheated water bath, set to whatever temperature is best suited to the item you're cooking. Without a vacuum sealer, you may need to add weights to the bag to get lighter items like vegetables to fully submerge; see detailed instructions in Tips for Submerging Vegetables without a Vacuum Sealer (page 130).

DONENESS

Your next question may well be: "How on earth do you expect me to know what temperature I should use?" The short answer is I don't—that's what this book is for! Each master recipe includes a specific temperature that has been painstakingly tested to achieve what I consider ideal results. And when relevant, I also tell you how to customize that temperature to suit your tastes.

Because sous vide won't give you the visual and tactile clues typical of conventional cooking techniques, there's no intuitive way of knowing when your food is done. That's why each master recipe also gives recommended minimum and maximum cooking times—for example, "1 hour (or up to 3 hours)." This isn't a margin of error, but rather a window of ideal doneness—your food will be perfectly cooked as soon as you've reached the minimum time and will remain pristine (getting slightly more tender as time goes by) until the maximum is reached. However, if you go beyond the limit, your food will gradually lose its prime texture and become mushy.

Most recipes have a big buffer zone, so there's no need to stress about exact timing. So if you need to run an errand, or you and the kids are late coming home, you can leave your water bath unattended—and your food won't over-cook or get cold. I've also included a Time and Temperature Cooking Guide (page 182) at the back of the book for you to reference whenever you're ready to branch out and cook foods beyond those featured in master recipes.

TABLE-EDGE METHOD

1.

2.

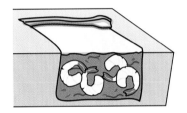

3.

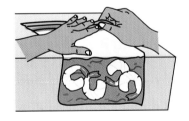

4.

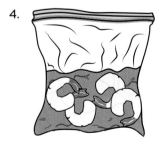

You'll note that the master recipes in this book use Celsius as the standard temperature scale for the water bath. The simple reason is that I think Celsius is easier to parse, with clearer, more regular increments—for example, medium rare steak at 55°C and chicken breast at 63°C versus 131°F or 145.4°F. In the instances where I call for conventional cooking methods such as frying or baking, I've called for Fahrenheit, as that's the only option for most American appliances.

STEP 3: FINISHING

Once your food is cooked and out of the bath, now comes the exciting bit—the final steps to transform it into something truly delicious. At this point, your master recipe ingredient has only bare-bones seasoning, so this is the time to bring in some personality. Throughout the book I've used a wide variety of different seasoning and finishing approaches, from the most simple (sous vide shrimp are ready to eat as soon as they're cold, to be paired with a simple classic cocktail sauce) to more involved preparations (like battering and deep-frying cauliflower before tossing it in a flavor-packed Sino-Indian Manchurian sauce). Whether the recipe calls for grilling, pan-searing, roasting, or frying, over- or undercooking aren't concerns. The goal is simply to enhance flavor or texture (or both) and heating it through to make an enticing final dish.

PAT IT DRY

In most cases, I instruct you to remove the cooked main ingredient from its bag and pat it dry with paper towels (the exception being dishes calling for the ingredient to be added directly to a soup or stew). Removing moisture from the food's surface makes it easier for rubs and other coatings to adhere, and promotes crisping and browning when searing.

SAVE THE LIQUID

In almost every case, the main ingredient will release some liquid into the bag as it cooks. I refer to this as the "cooking juices" (other recipes sometimes refer to this as "purge," which is just gross). In many recipes, such as the Balsamic Teriyaki Mushroom Skewers (page 152), this liquid is set aside and then incorporated into a sauce later in the recipe. In recipes that don't call for this, I still encourage you to strain and reserve the liquid to use for whenever you want to add a boost of flavor to a dish (this is especially the case for slow-cooked meats). Simply bring the liquid to a boil in a small pot on the stove or in a microwave-safe bowl, remove it from the heat, and strain it through a fine-mesh strainer into an air-tight container (discarding the coagulated protein that formed). Strained cooking juices can be stored in the refrigerator for up to a week or in the freezer for up to two months.

GIVE IT A REST

Most conventional meat recipes call for you to let the meat rest after cooking. The reason behind this is both to allow for carryover cooking and to let the meat juices redistribute before slicing, so that they don't pour out onto your cutting board. Carryover cooking isn't relevant to sous vide cooking, since your meat is already evenly cooked throughout—but resting does have a useful role when it comes to searing. In the master recipes, you'll see that I call for a brief resting time after cooking sous vide if you're going to use the meats right away for a spin-off recipe. This allows time for juices to redistribute, but more important, it lets the food cool slightly so that it doesn't overcook when you administer the final dose of heat to form a sear. Once seared, an additional brief rest ensures redistribution of the juices and heat if your meat is going to be sliced.

FOOD SAFETY

When it comes to food safety, sous vide is very much the same as any other cooking method. The primary concern for any type of food safety is to prevent the growth of pathogens (harmful bacteria), and sous vide is no exception. In fact, sous vide is no more dangerous to your health than any traditional cooking method—and when used properly (as in the case of pasteurization), it's actually safer. So put your mind at ease and cook boldly while bearing in mind some food-safety basics.

STAY OUT OF THE DANGER ZONE

Foods that are hospitable to bacterial growth (meats, seafood, vegetables—basically all fresh foods) can't be kept too long at the so-called "temperature danger zone," where they multiply fastest. The temperature range most often given for food safety defines this danger zone as between 4.4°C (40°F), below which bacteria grow very slowly, and 60°C (140°F), above which most bacteria are killed. It is advised that foods remain in this range for no longer than 2 hours.

That said, a few master recipes in this book call for food to be cooked to below 60°C (140°F), but don't be alarmed: that 60°C mark is more of a rule of thumb than a definitive line in the sand. The precise, even heating of sous vide means that you can cook just below that line without creating additional risk. Eliminating pathogens is a function of both time and temperature, meaning that food held at a temperature of 55°C (131°F) for many hours can be effectively pasteurized—that is, over 99.9 percent of the bacteria are destroyed. As the temperature rises, the time it takes to pasteurize decreases, which means that cooking at 63°C (145.4°F) for an hour is more than enough time to make any of the chicken recipes safe to eat.

If this seems like a lot of numbers to memorize, rest assured: all of the recipes in this book were written with safety in mind. Beyond that, be aware that most immersion circulators have a built-in function to indicate when the water is below a safe temperature.

TAKE COVER

For master recipes that feature longer cooking times, like the Braised Beef (page 86), or require a higher temperature, like the Root Vegetables (page 132) and other vegetables, I recommend covering the top of your water bath to minimize evaporation and keep your circulator chugging along. To accomplish this, simply cross 2 sheets of aluminum foil or plastic wrap, leaving an open wedge where they meet so your device can stick through. (Avoid an airtight seal, as condensation could damage your machine). If you don't cover your water bath for longer cooking times, check on it every few hours to make sure the water level hasn't dropped too low. If the water level has fallen below the machine's minimum, or if the bag is no longer submerged, simply add more water. Although the additional water will briefly lower the overall temperature slightly, don't worry. Over the course of a long cooking time, that fluctuation will have a negligible impact.

THE TRUTH ABOUT PLASTIC

Another common (and understandable) question is whether cooking in plastic is safe. The answer is an emphatic yes. Modern food-safe plastic bags are made from material that is not harmful when heated. With sous vide cooking, the plastic that touches your food is made only of inert polyethylene. There are no small-molecule additives like BPA and phthalates that have been used in other containers and have caused concern about potential estrogen-like effects when they leach into foods. As long as you're using freezer-safe bags, which are tested to be safely heated, there's no need to worry.

STORING SOUS VIDE FOOD SAFELY

Cooking your food sous vide will extend its shelf life, yet the same com-monsense rules that apply to storing any ingredient also hold true for food that has been cooked sous vide: discoloration and bubbling (for example, the bag begins to inflate) are sure signs that your food has begun to spoil. If when you open the bag you notice any rancid, sour, or otherwise funky smell, that's another indication that your food has passed edibility (the exception is cauliflower, which has a naturally sulfurous smell when cooked). Minimizing the time window for bacterial growth is the key to safe sous vide cooking. For that reason, if you're going to refrigerate food cooked sous vide (as opposed to eating it immediately), I always recommend rapidly chilling it in an ice water bath first. Since the format of this book presumes that you will cook the master recipes ahead of time and prepare a spin-off dish at some point later in the week, the recipes instruct you to chill your bagged food in a water bath before storing. (If you choose to make the spin-off dish in one go—that is, from water bath to finished dish—you can skip this step.)

BATCH COOKING, STORING, AND THAWING

The entire premise of this book is to show you how sous vide can be used as an effective tool for streamlining your everyday cooking routine by preparing your main ingredients ahead of time. Here are a few additional tips to get the most out of this approach.

COOKING IN BATCHES

Since cooking multiple pounds of chicken breasts or shrimp doesn't take any more time than cooking a single portion, sous vide is an ideal method for batch cooking. While most of the master recipes in this book make approxi-mately 4 to 6 servings, all can be doubled or even tripled, so long as you have a large-enough water bath to fit all the bags and still allow adequate water circulation. In most cases, you'll need to use multiple bags; as a general rule of thumb, approximately 2 pounds of protein can fit comfortably into a

CHILLING PROPERLY: THE ICE WATER BATH METHOD

When I talk about using an ice water bath to chill food, I don't mean a few ice cubes floating in a bowl. To cool down food efficiently, use the coldest water possible, which means adding enough ice to bring the water all the way down to 32°F. Adding salt lowers the freezing point of water, making an even colder bath possible. The following instructions will produce an ice water bath ideal for chilling your sous vide foods, but do not feel obliged to follow it slavishly. Instead, think of the ratios as a rough guide and of adding salt as a best-case option.

To make a proper ice water bath, fill a large bowl with ice cubes and add cold tap water equal to about half the volume of ice. Add kosher salt equal to about one-fourth the volume of water and stir until the mixture is very cold (it will be around 28°F in about 30 seconds). The ratio is 1 part salt, 4 parts water, and 8 parts ice, so for a 4-quart bowl filled with ice, add 8 cups cold tap water and 2 cups kosher salt.

1-gallon bag. You can also double or triple the spin-off recipes, applying the same logic you would for any conventional recipe, using a large-enough pan or multiple ones as necessary. The preparation time and instructions will be the same.

Because different kinds of protein and vegetables call for different cooking temperatures, I generally discourage cooking disparate items in the same water bath at the same time. (In the case of the chicken breast and poached eggs master recipes, both call for cooking at 63°C (145.4°F) for 1 hour, so feel free to place a few eggs directly into your water bath along with your bagged chicken). If you want to prepare multiple master recipes in the same session, I recommend cooking each one separately: start with the item that requires the higher cooking temperature first, then remove the bag, lower the heat, and cook the next item. For instance, if you want to prepare a week's worth of chicken thighs, shrimp, and pork loin, set your water bath to 65°C (149°F), cook the thighs for 90 minutes, adjust the temperature to 60°C (140°F), cook the bagged shrimp for 30 minutes, remove, then lower to 58°C (136.4°F) and cook the pork for 1 hour. Remember, you'll need to chill each item in an ice water bath after its cooked, but you can simply add more ice as you go to keep it sufficiently cold.

STORING AND REHEATING COOKED FOOD

Batch cooking staples like chicken thighs and skirt steak sous vide not only helps you save time and money, but it also helps prevent wasting food. It's a great way to utilize that 10-pound bag of Costco chicken breasts, since foods cooked in sealed bags have a far greater shelf life than leaving them raw or cooking them by conventional methods. Raw seafood won't keep for longer than a day or two—but cooked and sealed, it will keep for a week. By removing the air from the environment, you're killing the surface bacteria that causes food to spoil. For this reason, I also recommend you chill your food after it's been cooked and not open up the bag until you're ready to use it.

When it's time to prepare a spin-off dish, reheat the bagged, already-cooked master recipe in a water bath set to the same temperature you initially used and heat for half the recommended minimum cooking time, then proceed according to the instructions, using the master recipe component as if it were just cooked. For instance, the Chicken Breast master (page 42) calls for cooking at 63°C (145.4°F) for 1 hour; to make Baked Chicken Parmesan (page 47), reheat the bagged, cooked breasts at 63°C for 30 minutes before layering them with marinara and cheese and baking.

THAWING AND COOKING FROM FROZEN

In general, I recommend thawing frozen raw food overnight in the fridge rather than cooking sous vide from frozen. If you do opt to cook from frozen, my rule of thumb is double the recommended minimum time, which will compensate for the initial drop in temperature of the water bath and still ensure that the food is cooked all the way through. This method is less reliable for items that require longer cooking times, such as the Slow-Cooked Pork (page 68) or Braised Beef (page 86); anything that requires more than 3 hours of cooking really ought to be thawed first.

The freezer, however, can be your friend when it comes to storing already-cooked sous vide foods and ready-to-go master recipes. To use in spin-off recipes, allow them to thaw overnight in the fridge. If you're absolutely pressed for time, reheat them in a water bath at the same temperature and time as originally called for, and then proceed as instructed, as if it was just cooked.

ESSENTIAL EQUIPMENT

Now that you know the basics of sous vide cooking, it's time to get started. The good news is that very little equipment is required, and most of it is probably already in your kitchen. Aside from an immersion circulator (any sous vide device will work) you will need the following items.

A LARGE CONTAINER FOR YOUR WATER BATH. Any standard 8- to 12-quart stockpot or canning pot will work fine. You can also pick up a 12-quart square polycarbonate food storage container at a restaurant supply store or online for about twenty-five dollars—just confirm that it can be safely heated up to 95°C (203°F).

PLASTIC BAGS. Commercially available 1-gallon freezer-safe ziplock bags do a good job of eliminating air and are completely safe (see page 12). Just make sure the bags have a double seal (not a sliding closure) and are labeled "freezer" or "storage," as these are also designed to stand up to use in a microwave, where the temperatures are much higher than in sous vide cooking. Plant-based bags won't work, as they will fall apart when heated, but if you're concerned about adding more plastic to the environment, purchase reusable pouches designed specifically for sous vide, or simply wash out and reuse your used ziplock bags.

MASON JARS. Small glass jars are handy to use when you're making single-serving items that you want to serve in the same vessel you've cooked them in, such as egg bites, liquor infusions, and custard-based desserts like pot de crème. Note that cooking in glass vessels requires some special attention. If

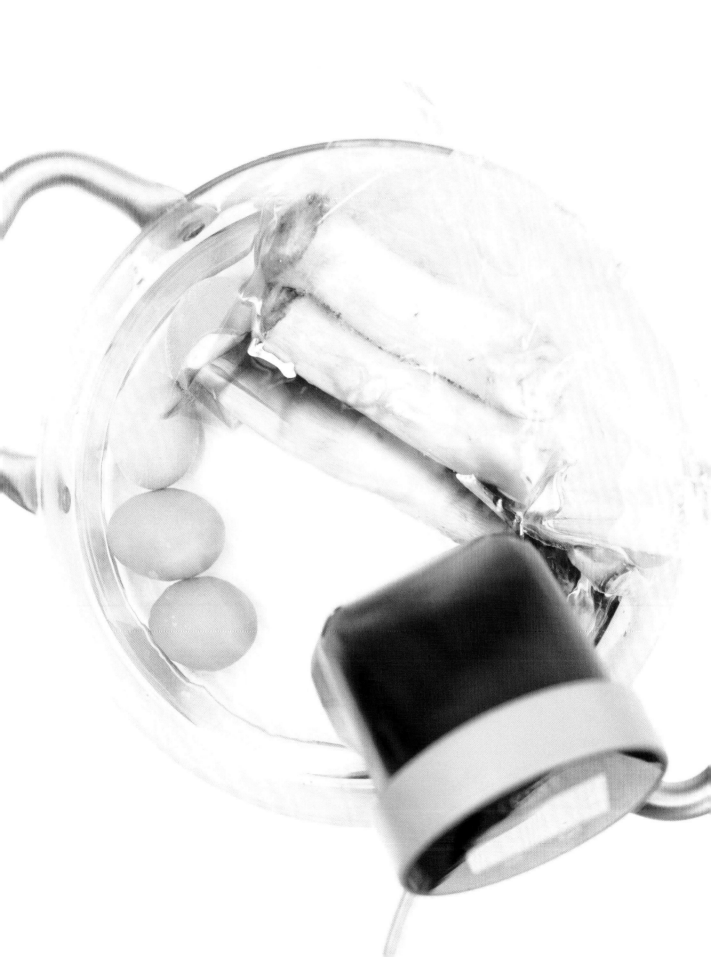

you add jars to a water bath after it has reached 80°C or higher, the glass may crack due to heat shock. To avoid that, place the jars in the water bath before it's hot. In the case of egg bites, since they are cooked at 75°C, there's no need to put the jars in the water bath early.

SMALL WEIGHTS AND CLIPS. One- to two-pound weights such as stainless steel spoons, dull butter knives, or pie weights come in handy for preventing ziplock-sealed bags from floating to the top of the water bath. Binder clips and cooking racks are also helpful to keep the bags in place. For detailed instructions on how to use them, see page 130.

TONGS AND LADLES. These come in handy when removing bags, jars, or whole eggs from the hot water bath.

CAST-IRON SKILLET, GRILL PAN, AND/OR A KITCHEN BLOWTORCH. To achieve that all-important, flavorful brown crust on a steak or grill marks on a pork chop, you need a fast heat source. Hard-core gadget lovers can splurge on a kitchen blowtorch (available for under forty dollars), but for everyday meals like the ones included in this book, a quick sear in a cast-iron skillet or grill pan works just fine.

VACUUM SEALER. Though not a requirement, if you plan on cooking a lot of vegetables sous vide, this will make your life infinitely easier. Not only do vacuum sealers remove the most air possible, which helps your bags stay submerged, but the firmer seal increases the length of time you can store your food in the fridge or freezer without worrying about things like freezer burn. Models range from expensive, large chamber vacuum sealers that pull out the oxygen with a powerful vacuum to smaller edge-style models that draw out the air from the open end of the bag. The affordable edge-style models such as FoodSaver will get the job done. Note that most vacuum sealers don't work well for bags filled with a large quantity of liquid. If you're adding a sauce or marinade to your bag and your machine doesn't have a liquid setting, use the override setting—otherwise the machine will suck out all the liquid and make a giant mess. If your machine doesn't have an override setting, freeze your marinade or sauce in an ice cube tray or small shallow pan before adding it to the bag and sealing.

***

Now that we've covered the basics, you have all you need to dive into sous vide cooking. Whether you faithfully follow my recipes or explore variations of your own design, my hope is that this book will show you that sous vide is a wonderful ally for getting incredible food on your table any night of the week. Now start your immersion circulators and get cooking!

TIPS FOR GETTING
YOUR BAG TO SINK

Precise temperature regulation is critical for safe sous vide cooking, so it's essential that bagged food is fully immersed in hot circulating water as it cooks. If a bag floats at the water's surface or lays flat at the bottom, you risk exposing a portion of the bagged food to temperatures low enough for bacterial growth. Sealing foods in ziplock bags has a slight disadvantage from vacuum sealing in that they are more prone to float. This is particularly true of lightweight vegetables such as cauliflower and mushrooms, which are less dense than water and therefore naturally buoyant. Other times, it's the gas that gets released during the cooking process that causes bags to float.

To avoid this, remove as much air as possible when sealing (see page 12 for instructions) so that the bag stays below the water surface. If necessary, place something above or inside your bag to prevent it from floating.

INTERNAL WEIGHTS. The simplest way to submerge your bag is by placing a small amount of weight—such as a couple of stainless steel spoons, a few dull butter knives, or a handful of pie weights—directly into the bottom of the bag. (Avoid using anything sharp to prevent puncturing the bag.)

EXTERNAL WEIGHTS. You can also use a large bull-dog or binder clip to clamp the bag to the side of your pot, or put the clip directly onto the bottom of the bag and slip a spoon through the mouth of the clip to keep it weighed down. Other external weighting tricks include placing tongs or an expand-able metal steamer over your bag to hold it in place, or adding a rack (either one specifically designed for sous vide or a small metal lid holder) into your cook-ing vessel and slipping the bagged food in the slots.

Channel your inner MacGyver and play around until you find what works. Whatever you choose, the important thing is that the water is able to freely circulate around the bag for the duration of cook-ing, so be sure it doesn't lie flat at the bottom of the cooking vessel or flush against the side. For more tips on how to submerge your bags properly, see page 130).

A NOTE ON SALT

Salt is inarguably the most important seasoning at a cook's disposal. Not only is it one of the four basic tastes (five, if you include umami), but it also improves overall flavor by enhancing aromas and masking bitter flavors. Salt also penetrates into food, which helps proteins maintain moisture and increases our perception of juiciness, which is why I almost always call for salting food before cooking sous vide. Here are a few pointers for how I season my foods with salt.

SEASON TO TASTE

Most of the master recipes in this book call for seasoning "to taste," but don't take that too literally. For obvious reasons, I don't expect you to take a lick of your raw chicken to determine if you've used an adequate amount of salt. Learning to season your food properly is a product of experience, but also of personal taste—one person's bland can be another's salt lick.

CONSIDER THE TYPE OF SALT

The salt measurements in this book call for Diamond Crystal kosher salt, which is affordable and widely available. I like it because its light, flaky texture makes it easy to gauge quantity and distribute evenly over the surface of meat when using your fingertips. Because it's relatively fine, it also dissolves more readily than other types of salt. Other brands of kosher salt, such as Morton's, can be as much as twice as dense—meaning an equal volume is roughly double the quantity of salt—and table salt and fine sea salt can be even denser. When calling for finishing salt, which is added to a dish just before serving, I recommend extra-flaky salts such as Maldon or fleur de sel, which add a pleasant salty crunch.

SEASON EVENLY

For the best results in any recipe, seasoning evenly is key. The best way to accomplish this is as follows: using your fingertips, grab a generous pinch of salt, and hold your hand 10 to 12 inches above the item you're seasoning. Move your hand back and forth while letting the salt fall—the height gives the salt space to scatter and coat the food surface evenly. Flip and repeat for the other side, and don't worry if some of the salt is left behind on your work surface.

HOW MUCH?

Different food items require different quantities of salt. Meats like beef and pork can handle heavier seasoning than lighter proteins like chicken, which in turn can handle more than delicate fish and shellfish (ditto veggies). Furthermore, the more fat an item has, the more salt is needed for the best-tasting food—for example, chicken thigh takes more salt than chicken breast. Bear this in mind when seasoning. Some items like fish benefit from a special salting approach like brining to improve texture (see page 113 for details).

DON'T OVERSALT

Remember, you can always add salt to a finished spin-off dish—but once added, it can't be removed. For that reason, when seasoning the master recipes in this book, err on the side of restraint and salt lightly.

EGGS

POACHED EGGS

When it comes to my absolute favorite food to cook sous vide, the chicken will have to wait its turn—the egg comes first. If you've never had the joy of biting into a sous vide egg, be prepared to be dazzled. When slowly cooked at relatively low temperatures, eggs take on a singularly seductive texture— whites with a soft, cloudlike consistency envelop a slightly thickened yet still creamy yolk. The recipe below yields my ideal egg, similar to *onsen tamago* aka "hot spring eggs," a centuries-old Japanese method for cooking eggs in geothermal vents. Luckily we can now reproduce the custardy consistency of *onsen* eggs in the comfort of our twenty-first-century kitchens.

Although 63°C (145.4°F) is my favorite temperature for poaching eggs, I encourage you to find your own. Eggs are extremely responsive to temperature, making them remarkably suitable to the precise temperature control of sous vide cooking. Just one or two degrees Celsius causes a dramatic difference in the way cooked eggs turn out—and timing plays a part as well. So, if after your first foray following the instructions below, you prefer your whites slightly softer, try cooking at 62°C (143.6°F) or for 15 minutes fewer. Want things a little firmer? Try 64°C (147.2°F), which will make the yolk thick and spreadable, like tempered butter. Raise the heat to 65°C (149°F) and you'll end up with a yolk that resembles a hard-cooked egg, though the whites will still be quite soft. In other words, go ahead and *eggs*periment!

Don't be put off by thought of spending an hour to prepare these otherworldly poached eggs. All the cooking time is hands-off. And by preparing a bunch in advance, you'll have a steady supply in your fridge any time you want to whip up an eggy indulgence, be it Middle Eastern– inspired baked eggs, a brunch-worthy asparagus Benedict, or simply cracked on top of your favorite dish to gild it with a golden yolky stream.

Preheat the water bath to 63°C (145.4°F).

When the water reaches the target temperature, using a slotted spoon, carefully lower the whole eggs directly into the water bath and cook for 1 hour (or up to 2 hours).

Remove the eggs from the water bath. Chill the eggs in an ice water bath (page 18) for 10 minutes before refrigerating. Cooked eggs can be kept in the refrigerator for 2 weeks or more.

If using right away: Set the eggs aside at room temperature for at least 15 minutes, or up to 1 hour, before proceeding. For recipes where an additional cooking step isn't necessary (as in the Asparagus Benedict, page 33), the eggs can be kept warm and ready to serve by lowering the water temperature to 60°C (140°F) for up to 2 hours.

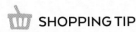

SHOPPING TIP

Even though eggs come naturally presealed, freshness still matters. Assuming you don't have an urban chicken coop to pull from, it's best to cook your eggs as soon after buying them as you can. Shells are slightly porous, so over time the whites will begin to thin and be slightly runnier when cooked. The recipes in this section call for large eggs cooked straight from the fridge, but any size or type of egg will work—including just-laid ones. There's no need to adjust the temperature, though smaller eggs cook slightly more quickly.

ADDITIONAL SPIN-OFF IDEAS

Crack a warm egg over your favorite lo mein or simple Italian pasta—the runny yolks are wickedly good for making spaghetti carbonara even more eggy and luxurious. Likewise, add these luscious eggs, warm or cold, to a bowl of ramen or any soup when you want to add a little richness.

HOW TO MIMIC THE TEXTURE OF A FRIED OR POACHED EGG

It's hard to beat the silky consistency of a sous vide egg, but sometimes a firmer texture is the best fit for a particular recipe. For this reason, I have provided instructions for replicating traditional poached and fried eggs in the Asparagus Benedict (page 33) and Kimchi Fried Rice (page 36) recipes, respectively. These additional cooking steps give the egg whites a firmer, more familiar texture, but precooking them sous vide still improves the texture of the yolk and makes the final step faster, more reliable, and simpler than the conventional method alone—the best of both worlds!

CRACKING A SOUS VIDE EGG

Cracking open a sous vide egg for the first time can be a bit surprising: although most of the white will be set, some of it will fall apart as loose curds. Don't worry—nothing has gone wrong with your egg! You just need to take some care when cracking it open. To remove a sous vide egg from its shell without breaking the fragile white, crack it against a solid, flat surface like a countertop (rather than the side of a bowl, which forces shell shards inward and can tear the white and potentially the yolk as well). Use one quick, firm strike to crack the egg, then, holding the egg over a bowl and using both hands, pull the shell apart in opposite directions, letting the egg drop gently into the bowl. Using a slotted spoon, lift the egg from the bowl, giving the spoon a little jiggle to make sure that all the unset white is left behind before serving.

EGGPLANT SHAKSHUKA

SERVES 4 TO 6

🕐 30 MINUTES

3 tablespoons extra-virgin olive oil

3 cloves garlic, thinly sliced

1 or 2 green or red chiles, such as Fresno or jalapeño, seeded if desired and chopped

1 yellow or white onion, cut into ¼-inch dice

1 pound eggplant (preferably Japanese), peeled and cut into ½-inch dice

Salt and freshly ground black pepper

1½ teaspoons ground cumin

1 tablespoon paprika

1 cup water or vegetable broth

1 (14-ounce) can crushed tomatoes or tomato puree

1 tablespoon freshly squeezed lemon juice

1 teaspoon finely grated lemon zest

4 to 8 MASTER RECIPE Poached Eggs (page 28), just cooked or straight from the fridge

¼ cup chopped Italian parsley or cilantro, or a mix, for garnish

Warm pita or toasted challah bread, for serving

What's for breakfast? Throughout much of the Middle East and northern Africa, the answer is *shakshuka*. Once you taste the combination of gooey eggs in a hearty spiced sauce (think of it as a ratatouille), you'll know why. There is a nearly infinite number of variations on *shakshuka*, but I think that the inclusion of eggplant compliments it perfectly. Though typically *shakshuka* is served as the first meal of the day, it also makes for a satisfying lunch or dinner—particularly if you serve it with plenty of warm bread to sop up the delicious sauce.

In a large shallow straight-sided frying pan or skillet with a matching lid, heat the olive oil over medium heat until shimmering. Add the garlic, chiles, and onion and cook, stirring frequently, until the onions turn translucent and begin to soften, 2 to 3 minutes. Add the eggplant and a pinch of salt. Continue to cook, stirring often, until the eggplant has softened and begun to brown in places (keep an eye on the garlic to make sure it's not getting too dark—lower the heat to medium-low if necessary), 4 to 5 minutes more.

Once the eggplant has softened, add the cumin and paprika and cook until the mixture is aromatic, about 30 seconds. Add the water and tomato and bring to a boil. Reduce the heat to a simmer and cook until the mixture is thickened enough to hold its shape somewhat, 3 to 5 minutes. Add the lemon juice and zest, and season to taste with salt and pepper. At this point, the sauce can be cooled and stored in an airtight container for up to a week before reheating to serve.

Using the back of a large wooden spoon or spoon-shaped rubber spatula, create 4 indents in the sauce large enough to hold the eggs.

Carefully crack a poached egg into a bowl (see page 29 for proper cracking technique) and, using a slotted spoon, gently place it into an indent you've created, leaving the unset whites behind. Repeat with the rest of the eggs. Cover the pan, decrease the heat to low, and cook until the egg whites have begun to set and turn completely opaque, but the yolks remain runny, 2 to 3 minutes. (If you're using eggs straight from the refrigerator, add an additional 1 to 2 minutes to ensure the eggs are heated through.)

Use a large serving spoon to scoop the eggs and surrounding sauce among four shallow bowls or plates, sprinkle the parsley or cilantro on top, and serve with warm bread.

SHOPPING TIP

Even though eggs come naturally presealed, freshness still matters. Assuming you don't have an urban chicken coop to pull from, it's best to cook your eggs as soon after buying them as you can. Shells are slightly porous, so over time the whites will begin to thin and be slightly runnier when cooked. The recipes in this section call for large eggs cooked straight from the fridge, but any size or type of egg will work—including just-laid ones. There's no need to adjust the temperature, though smaller eggs cook slightly more quickly.

ADDITIONAL SPIN-OFF IDEAS

Crack a warm egg over your favorite lo mein or simple Italian pasta—the runny yolks are wickedly good for making spaghetti carbonara even more eggy and luxurious. Likewise, add these luscious eggs, warm or cold, to a bowl of ramen or any soup when you want to add a little richness.

HOW TO MIMIC THE TEXTURE OF A FRIED OR POACHED EGG

It's hard to beat the silky consistency of a sous vide egg, but sometimes a firmer texture is the best fit for a particular recipe. For this reason, I have provided instructions for replicating traditional poached and fried eggs in the Asparagus Benedict (page 33) and Kimchi Fried Rice (page 36) recipes, respectively. These additional cooking steps give the egg whites a firmer, more familiar texture, but precooking them sous vide still improves the texture of the yolk and makes the final step faster, more reliable, and simpler than the conventional method alone—the best of both worlds!

CRACKING A SOUS VIDE EGG

Cracking open a sous vide egg for the first time can be a bit surprising: although most of the white will be set, some of it will fall apart as loose curds. Don't worry—nothing has gone wrong with your egg! You just need to take some care when cracking it open. To remove a sous vide egg from its shell without breaking the fragile white, crack it against a solid, flat surface like a countertop (rather than the side of a bowl, which forces shell shards inward and can tear the white and potentially the yolk as well). Use one quick, firm strike to crack the egg, then, holding the egg over a bowl and using both hands, pull the shell apart in opposite directions, letting the egg drop gently into the bowl. Using a slotted spoon, lift the egg from the bowl, giving the spoon a little jiggle to make sure that all the unset white is left behind before serving.

EGGPLANT SHAKSHUKA

SERVES 4 TO 6

🕐 30 MINUTES

3 tablespoons extra-virgin olive oil

3 cloves garlic, thinly sliced

1 or 2 green or red chiles, such as Fresno or jalapeño, seeded if desired and chopped

1 yellow or white onion, cut into ¼-inch dice

1 pound eggplant (preferably Japanese), peeled and cut into ½-inch dice

Salt and freshly ground black pepper

1½ teaspoons ground cumin

1 tablespoon paprika

1 cup water or vegetable broth

1 (14-ounce) can crushed tomatoes or tomato puree

1 tablespoon freshly squeezed lemon juice

1 teaspoon finely grated lemon zest

4 to 8 MASTER RECIPE Poached Eggs (page 28), just cooked or straight from the fridge

¼ cup chopped Italian parsley or cilantro, or a mix, for garnish

Warm pita or toasted challah bread, for serving

What's for breakfast? Throughout much of the Middle East and northern Africa, the answer is *shakshuka*. Once you taste the combination of gooey eggs in a hearty spiced sauce (think of it as a ratatouille), you'll know why. There is a nearly infinite number of variations on *shakshuka*, but I think that the inclusion of eggplant compliments it perfectly. Though typically *shakshuka* is served as the first meal of the day, it also makes for a satisfying lunch or dinner—particularly if you serve it with plenty of warm bread to sop up the delicious sauce.

In a large shallow straight-sided frying pan or skillet with a matching lid, heat the olive oil over medium heat until shimmering. Add the garlic, chiles, and onion and cook, stirring frequently, until the onions turn translucent and begin to soften, 2 to 3 minutes. Add the eggplant and a pinch of salt. Continue to cook, stirring often, until the eggplant has softened and begun to brown in places (keep an eye on the garlic to make sure it's not getting too dark—lower the heat to medium-low if necessary), 4 to 5 minutes more.

Once the eggplant has softened, add the cumin and paprika and cook until the mixture is aromatic, about 30 seconds. Add the water and tomato and bring to a boil. Reduce the heat to a simmer and cook until the mixture is thickened enough to hold its shape somewhat, 3 to 5 minutes. Add the lemon juice and zest, and season to taste with salt and pepper. At this point, the sauce can be cooled and stored in an airtight container for up to a week before reheating to serve.

Using the back of a large wooden spoon or spoon-shaped rubber spatula, create 4 indents in the sauce large enough to hold the eggs.

Carefully crack a poached egg into a bowl (see page 29 for proper cracking technique) and, using a slotted spoon, gently place it into an indent you've created, leaving the unset whites behind. Repeat with the rest of the eggs. Cover the pan, decrease the heat to low, and cook until the egg whites have begun to set and turn completely opaque, but the yolks remain runny, 2 to 3 minutes. (If you're using eggs straight from the refrigerator, add an additional 1 to 2 minutes to ensure the eggs are heated through.)

Use a large serving spoon to scoop the eggs and surrounding sauce among four shallow bowls or plates, sprinkle the parsley or cilantro on top, and serve with warm bread.

 SHOPPING TIP

Even though eggs come naturally presealed, freshness still matters. Assuming you don't have an urban chicken coop to pull from, it's best to cook your eggs as soon after buying them as you can. Shells are slightly porous, so over time the whites will begin to thin and be slightly runnier when cooked. The recipes in this section call for large eggs cooked straight from the fridge, but any size or type of egg will work—including just-laid ones. There's no need to adjust the temperature, though smaller eggs cook slightly more quickly.

 ADDITIONAL SPIN-OFF IDEAS

Crack a warm egg over your favorite lo mein or simple Italian pasta—the runny yolks are wickedly good for making spaghetti carbonara even more eggy and luxurious. Likewise, add these luscious eggs, warm or cold, to a bowl of ramen or any soup when you want to add a little richness.

 HOW TO MIMIC THE TEXTURE OF A FRIED OR POACHED EGG

It's hard to beat the silky consistency of a sous vide egg, but sometimes a firmer texture is the best fit for a particular recipe. For this reason, I have provided instructions for replicating traditional poached and fried eggs in the Asparagus Benedict (page 33) and Kimchi Fried Rice (page 36) recipes, respectively. These additional cooking steps give the egg whites a firmer, more familiar texture, but precooking them sous vide still improves the texture of the yolk and makes the final step faster, more reliable, and simpler than the conventional method alone—the best of both worlds!

 CRACKING A SOUS VIDE EGG

Cracking open a sous vide egg for the first time can be a bit surprising: although most of the white will be set, some of it will fall apart as loose curds. Don't worry—nothing has gone wrong with your egg! You just need to take some care when cracking it open. To remove a sous vide egg from its shell without breaking the fragile white, crack it against a solid, flat surface like a countertop (rather than the side of a bowl, which forces shell shards inward and can tear the white and potentially the yolk as well). Use one quick, firm strike to crack the egg, then, holding the egg over a bowl and using both hands, pull the shell apart in opposite directions, letting the egg drop gently into the bowl. Using a slotted spoon, lift the egg from the bowl, giving the spoon a little jiggle to make sure that all the unset white is left behind before serving.

EGGPLANT SHAKSHUKA

SERVES 4 TO 6

🕐 30 MINUTES

3 tablespoons extra-virgin olive oil

3 cloves garlic, thinly sliced

1 or 2 green or red chiles, such as Fresno or jalapeño, seeded if desired and chopped

1 yellow or white onion, cut into ¼-inch dice

1 pound eggplant (preferably Japanese), peeled and cut into ½-inch dice

Salt and freshly ground black pepper

1½ teaspoons ground cumin

1 tablespoon paprika

1 cup water or vegetable broth

1 (14-ounce) can crushed tomatoes or tomato puree

1 tablespoon freshly squeezed lemon juice

1 teaspoon finely grated lemon zest

4 to 8 MASTER RECIPE Poached Eggs (page 28), just cooked or straight from the fridge

¼ cup chopped Italian parsley or cilantro, or a mix, for garnish

Warm pita or toasted challah bread, for serving

What's for breakfast? Throughout much of the Middle East and northern Africa, the answer is *shakshuka*. Once you taste the combination of gooey eggs in a hearty spiced sauce (think of it as a ratatouille), you'll know why. There is a nearly infinite number of variations on *shakshuka*, but I think that the inclusion of eggplant compliments it perfectly. Though typically *shakshuka* is served as the first meal of the day, it also makes for a satisfying lunch or dinner—particularly if you serve it with plenty of warm bread to sop up the delicious sauce.

In a large shallow straight-sided frying pan or skillet with a matching lid, heat the olive oil over medium heat until shimmering. Add the garlic, chiles, and onion and cook, stirring frequently, until the onions turn translucent and begin to soften, 2 to 3 minutes. Add the eggplant and a pinch of salt. Continue to cook, stirring often, until the eggplant has softened and begun to brown in places (keep an eye on the garlic to make sure it's not getting too dark—lower the heat to medium-low if necessary), 4 to 5 minutes more.

Once the eggplant has softened, add the cumin and paprika and cook until the mixture is aromatic, about 30 seconds. Add the water and tomato and bring to a boil. Reduce the heat to a simmer and cook until the mixture is thickened enough to hold its shape somewhat, 3 to 5 minutes. Add the lemon juice and zest, and season to taste with salt and pepper. At this point, the sauce can be cooled and stored in an airtight container for up to a week before reheating to serve.

Using the back of a large wooden spoon or spoon-shaped rubber spatula, create 4 indents in the sauce large enough to hold the eggs.

Carefully crack a poached egg into a bowl (see page 29 for proper cracking technique) and, using a slotted spoon, gently place it into an indent you've created, leaving the unset whites behind. Repeat with the rest of the eggs. Cover the pan, decrease the heat to low, and cook until the egg whites have begun to set and turn completely opaque, but the yolks remain runny, 2 to 3 minutes. (If you're using eggs straight from the refrigerator, add an additional 1 to 2 minutes to ensure the eggs are heated through.)

Use a large serving spoon to scoop the eggs and surrounding sauce among four shallow bowls or plates, sprinkle the parsley or cilantro on top, and serve with warm bread.

Eggplant varieties with fewer seeds work best in this recipe, so I suggest seeking out the slender Japanese variety. If you can't find them, pick the smallest, firmest eggplant you can find, which indicates that the seeds have not fully developed.

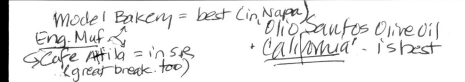

Model Bakery = best (in Napa) Eng. Muf
Cafe Attila = in S.R. (great break. too)
Olio Santos Olive Oil + California' - is best

ASPARAGUS BENEDICT

Mrs. Dash on asparagus – 400° oven – 10–15 min

SERVES 4
30 MINUTES

10 MASTER RECIPE Poached Eggs (page 28), just cooked or straight from the fridge

ASPARAGUS

1 bunch medium-thick asparagus (about 1 pound; spears about ½ inch thick), tough stems trimmed off

1 tablespoon extra-virgin olive oil

Salt and freshly ground black pepper

MALTAISE SAUCE

1 to 2 teaspoons white wine vinegar or lemon juice

2 tablespoons freshly squeezed orange juice (preferably blood orange), about 1 medium orange
Cara Cara oranges = sweeter

8 tablespoons (1 stick) unsalted butter
don't let it bubble + brown

1 teaspoon finely grated orange zest (preferably blood orange)

Salt

Pinch of red pepper flakes or cayenne, plus more for garnish

4 English muffins or biscuits, homemade (page 175) or store-bought, halved

8 slices smoked salmon or prosciutto (optional)

2 tablespoons chopped chives, tarragon, or parsley, or a mix, for garnish

The idea for this dish comes from the south of France, where *sauce Maltaise*, a variant of hollandaise made even more luscious with the addition of blood orange, is served as the perfect complement to asparagus. I've taken the liberty of translating that idea into the more familiar format of eggs Benedict, but I encourage you to try this dish as a lighter lunch or dinner—leave out the English muffin and serve the sauce and poached eggs over whole asparagus, perhaps with a side salad. In either case, the addition of prosciutto or smoked salmon is totally optional, but either pairs deliciously with the dish.

This recipe calls for 10 precooked 63°C (145.4°F) eggs, 2 of which need to be warm to make the sauce. You can either cook the eggs immediately before you start preparing this recipe and then lower the heat to 60°C (140°F) to keep them warm (for up to 2 hours), or you can reheat the eggs from cold, in which case you'll need to preheat the water bath to 60°C and warm them for 15 minutes before proceeding with the recipe. Alternatively, you can quickly poach them just before serving (see Cooking Tip on page 34). *

If using just-cooked eggs, keep them warm for up to 2 hours by lowering the water bath temperature to 60°C (140°F). *

If reheating eggs from the fridge, heat the water bath to 60°C (140°F), then place the eggs in the bath. Heat for at least 15 minutes or up to 2 hours before making the Maltaise.

PREPARE THE ASPARAGUS: Heat a grill pan over medium-high heat. On a plate or in a shallow bowl, toss the asparagus with the olive oil, salt, and pepper to coat. Add the asparagus to the grill pan and cook for 2 to 3 minutes or until lightly charred in places, then flip and cook an additional 2 to 3 minutes, until the other side has charred and the asparagus is just barely tender. Transfer to a cutting board and cut the asparagus through the middle (crosswise). Set aside.

MAKE THE MALTAISE: Crack 2 of the warmed poached eggs into a bowl, then use a slotted spoon to transfer them into a blender, leaving behind any egg white that doesn't cling to the yolk. Add 1 teaspoon of the vinegar, along with the orange juice to the blender and blend on low until the mixture is foamy, about 30 seconds. In a small saucepan, melt the butter over medium heat until it just begins to bubble but not brown. Immediately pour the hot butter into the blender in a slow, steady stream, keeping the blender running on low the entire time. When all of the butter is added, the mixture should be satiny and thick enough to coat the back of a spoon. ~~orange zest, cayenne~~

Warm Eng. muf (or slightly toast)

CONTINUED ›

ASPARAGUS BENEDICT
CONTINUED

Add the orange zest, salt, and additional vinegar to taste, and finish with a pinch of red pepper flakes or cayenne. If not serving immediately, cover the blender and set aside in a warm place. Toast your biscuits, if desired.

ASSEMBLE THE SANDWICHES: Divide the muffins or biscuit halves among four plates, cut side up. Place a slice of salmon onto each, and top with 3 to 5 grilled asparagus pieces.

Carefully crack a poached egg into a small bowl (see page 29 for proper cracking technique) and, using a slotted spoon, transfer the egg to the top of the asparagus, leaving behind any unset whites. (If you prefer firmer whites, see Cooking Tip below.) Repeat with the rest of the eggs. Spoon the sauce generously over each egg, sprinkle with the herbs and a pinch of red pepper flakes on top, and serve immediately. (Mimosas optional but recommended!)

If you prefer your egg whites with a more traditional poached texture, reheat them immediately before serving in simmering salted water for 1 to 2 minutes, or until the whites have set and the eggs are heated through. (Use this same method anytime you want a slightly firmer egg.) However, the 2 eggs used for the Maltaise sauce should be left in the shell and cooked for only 30 seconds, so that they're just reheated, without the white coagulating.

KIMCHI FRIED RICE

SERVES 4
🕐 20 MINUTES

¾ to 1½ cups kimchi, packed, coarsely chopped

1 to 2 tablespoons gochujang (depending on how spicy you like it), or 2 teaspoons Sriracha mixed with 1 teaspoon sugar or honey

1 tablespoon soy sauce, plus more as needed

3 tablespoons unsalted butter or canola or other neutral vegetable oil

3 green onions, thinly sliced, dark green parts reserved for garnish

4 cups cooked and cooled rice (preferably short or medium grain)

2 teaspoons toasted sesame oil

4 MASTER RECIPE Poached Eggs (page 28), just cooked or straight from the fridge

2 tablespoons roasted nori (seaweed) flakes, for garnish

1 tablespoon toasted sesame seeds, for garnish

How do I take my near-boundless love for fried rice to the next level? By combining it with another love of mine—kimchi, the tangy, spicy fermented cabbage that is the heart of Korean cuisine. Typical of Korean home cooking, where simplicity often belies a complex depth of flavor, this dish combines pantry ingredients with leftover rice to produce something extraordinary. As is always true with fried rice, it works best when the rice is cooked in advance and chilled, because the grains will stick less to the pan and each other. Gochujang, a Korean fermented soybean chile paste readily available at Asian markets, gives the dish its requisite heat. Butter, while not a traditional Korean ingredient, is increasingly common in modern Korean cooking, and its richness is a wonderful contrast to the lactic acid tang of kimchi. Once you try this beloved comfort food, you may find yourself cooking extra rice for other meals as an excuse to make this dish.

Before measuring the kimchi, use your hands to squeeze out as much liquid as possible into a bowl or measuring cup. Discard all but ¼ cup of the liquid. In a small bowl, whisk together the kimchi liquid, gochujang, and soy sauce. Set aside.

In a large wok or sauté pan, melt 2 tablespoons of the butter over medium-high heat until sizzling. Add the chopped kimchi and green onion (white and light green parts) and sauté, stirring frequently, until the kimchi and green onion have begun to brown, 3 to 4 minutes. Add the rice and drizzle it with the sesame oil, using a wooden spoon to break apart the rice and mix in the oil. Continue to cook, scraping the bottom of the pan with a wooden spoon to loosen the rice as it sticks to the pan, until the rice is heated through and beginning to brown in places, 2 to 5 minutes. Mix in the kimchi liquid mixture and cook for 1 to 2 minutes more, stirring constantly, until the liquid is incorporated. Remove from the heat and taste for seasoning, adding more soy sauce if desired.

In a separate nonstick pan, melt the remaining 1 tablespoon of butter over medium heat until sizzling. Carefully crack a poached egg into a small bowl (see page 29 for proper cracking technique) and, using a slotted spoon, transfer the egg to the skillet, leaving behind any unset whites. Repeat with the rest of the eggs. Cook until the edges of the egg whites begin to bubble and crisp, 1 to 2 minutes. If the eggs are coming straight from the fridge, turn the heat to low and cover the pan, cooking for 2 to 3 minutes more, until the eggs are warmed through—the tops should be just warm to the touch.

Divide the kimchi rice among four bowls and, using a spatula, remove each fried egg from the pan and place it on top of the rice. Sprinkle with the reserved green onion, toasted nori, and sesame seeds and serve immediately.

This technique for reheating eggs in a frying pan results in a texture that mimics a traditional fried egg, making a lovely contrast between the silky center and the crispy edges. Use this same method anytime you want a fried egg.

EGG BITES

Both delicious and convenient, it's easy to see why sous vide egg bites have become so popular in coffee shops. These savory custards are akin to crust-free quiches or baked omelets, and they're a snap to make in advance and reheat, for a filling breakfast or a light lunch served over a green salad.

Egg bites can be endlessly customized. I've included a handful of suggestions below; use this recipe as a blueprint for any combination you like. Keep in mind that if you want to add veggies, you'll need to cook them and blot them dry before adding them to the custard; otherwise they'll release too much liquid and make the custard too watery.

SOUS VIDE COOKING TIME

🕐 45 minutes (or up to 75 minutes for slightly firmer custard)

ACTIVE COOKING TIME

🕐 10 minutes

4 large eggs

¼ cup heavy cream, whole milk, or whole milk yogurt

Generous pinch salt

Freshly ground white or black pepper

OPTIONAL FILLINGS

½ cup grated Gruyère

¼ cup cooked bacon, crumbled or cut into bits (about 2 ounces raw)

Pinch of nutmeg

1 teaspoon minced chives or parsley

½ cup smoked salmon, coarsely chopped

1 teaspoon minced chives or dill

½ cup sundried tomato, coarsely chopped

¼ cup crumbled fresh goat cheese (chèvre)

1 teaspoon thinly sliced basil or chopped parsley

½ cup cooked mushrooms, any type, thinly sliced (try my master recipe Mushrooms)

½ cup grated fontina or sliced brie

Preheat the water bath to 75°C (167°F). Grease 4 (4-ounce) mason jars with butter or cooking spray.

In a small bowl or 1-pint measuring cup, whisk together the eggs, cream, salt, and pepper to taste. Divide whatever fillings you like evenly among the greased jars and pour one-fourth of the egg mixture into each. Stir each mixture once or twice with a chopstick or small spoon to distribute the ingredients. Cover each jar with its fitted lid. Use your fingertips to screw on the lid, using only light pressure so that the lids are closed but not too tight.

When the water reaches the target temperature, using tongs, gently lower the sealed jars into the water bath. Cook for 45 minutes (or up to 75 minutes). Using tongs, remove the jars from the water bath and set them on a flat surface. Let the egg bites rest for 5 minutes, at which point they will be ready to serve or refrigerate for up to 10 days. (There's no need to chill them before refrigerating.)

If serving the egg bites immediately, simply eat them right from the jar or unmold. To unmold, remove the lid, run a thin-bladed paring knife or small offset spatula around the perimeter of the jar to loosen the custard, and then flip over onto a cutting board or counter and give the jar a firm tap. The bite should release from the jar after a few seconds but give it a gentle shake if it needs extra encouragement to drop. Transfer to a plate and dig in.

To reheat your egg bites from cold, unmold and place in a toaster oven at 350°F for 8 to 15 minutes until warmed through (a knife inserted into the center is a good way to test), or warm under a broiler for about 5 minutes. Ovens vary greatly so watch to make sure the tops don't burn.

Alternatively, you can reheat egg bites in a microwave before unmolding. Remove the lids from the jars and microwave, one at a time, for 30 seconds to 1 minute on high heat (the jar will be hot to the touch, and the eggs will have puffed somewhat and be warm on top). Eat directly from the jar or unmold following the instructions above.

This recipe is perfect for making larger batches and reheating throughout the week. You can easily double or triple this recipe—just make sure to increase the number of jars, rather than using larger jars, or the cooking time will be off.

CHICKEN

SOUS VIDE COOKING TIME
1 hour (or up to 5 hours)

———

4 boneless, skinless chicken
breasts, about 2 pounds

Salt

———

CHICKEN BREAST

The unassuming chicken breast has risen to the top of the ladder as America's default protein of choice. Its affordability, mild flavor, and healthy profile (low in fat, high in protein) make it endlessly versatile in the kitchen. That said, white meat has the potential to be bland, boring, and dry—all pitfalls I want to help you avoid. The very things that give chicken breast its broad appeal, namely its leanness and lack of connective tissue, are what make it prone to drying out. This recipe gives you a bare-bones template for making sure your chicken breast is always juicy. The precision of sous vide cooking ensures uniformly excellent results, so you never have to worry about under- or overcooking your chicken.

As for bland, I've banished any possibility of that as well, with a trio of crowd-pleasing spin-off dishes that deploy myriad seasonings and cooking techniques to import even more flavor and texture. Whether you serve your chicken breasts cold, tossed with a zingy carrot ginger dressing for a main-course salad, layered with marinara and mozzarella and then baked to cheesy perfection for a comforting chicken parm, or fried for the best damn chicken biscuit sandwich this side of the Mississippi, you'll never have to hear the exasperated refrain "chicken again?"

Preheat the water bath to 63°C (145.4°F).

Season the chicken breasts with salt and place in a 1-gallon freezer-safe ziplock bag or a vacuum seal bag. Arrange the breasts in a single layer with as little overlap as possible to ensure even cooking. Seal the bag using either the water displacement method (page 12) or a vacuum sealer.

When the water reaches the target temperature, lower the bagged chicken in the water bath (making sure the bag is fully submerged) and cook for 1 hour (or up to 5 hours).

Remove the bag from the water bath, transfer it to an ice water bath (see page 18), and chill until completely cold, about 15 minutes. Once cooked and chilled, the chicken can be refrigerated in the bag for up to 10 days.

Alternatively, if you plan on using the just-cooked chicken in a spin-off recipe right away, let it rest in the bag at room temperature for at least 10 minutes or up to 1 hour before proceeding.

 SHOPPING TIP

Chicken breasts vary widely in size; I've even seen some monsters that weighed in at over 1 pound. The recipes in this section were tested with 8-ounce breasts of approximately 1-inch thickness, and I encourage you to use the same. If you can find only very large breasts, I recommend cutting them in half horizontally to make 2 thinner cutlets. Or plan on adding 30 minutes of cooking time for every additional ½ inch of thickness to ensure they get fully cooked.

 COOKING TIP

My technique for sous vide chicken calls for it to be cooked at lower temperatures than conventional techniques, which means the protein responsible for producing pink juices won't be fully denatured (this is even more noticeable after chilling). Rest assured, the chicken will still be perfectly safe to eat, and any pinkness will disappear after you've finished it with conventional cooking techniques in the spin-off recipes.

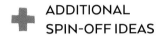 ADDITIONAL SPIN-OFF IDEAS

Add lean protein to your salads and stir-fries by thinly slicing these juicy precooked breasts, or brush them with your favorite glaze before grilling or broiling for white meat that's never dry or boring.

CHICKEN BISCUIT SANDWICHES

**SERVES 4 AS A MAIN DISH,
8 AS AN APPETIZER**
🕐 **20 MINUTES**

SLAW

¼ cup mayonnaise, homemade
(page 172) or store-bought

1 teaspoon whole grain or
other mustard

1 teaspoon apple cider vinegar

¼ teaspoon celery seed

Salt and freshly ground
black pepper

1½ cups cabbage, shredded or
thinly sliced

½ cup shredded carrots

1 MASTER RECIPE Chicken
Breast (page 42), just cooked or
straight from the fridge

2 tablespoons unsalted butter

1 clove garlic, minced

¼ cup honey

¼ cup hot sauce, such as Frank's

1 teaspoon fresh thyme leaves

8 large biscuits, homemade
(page 175) or store-bought,
split into halves

I don't need to explain the appeal of matching flaky, tender biscuits with succulent chicken—the combo speaks for itself. Typical versions of these sandwiches opt for fried chicken, but I find that pairing lightly seared chicken, buttery biscuits, and crunchy slaw with a sweet and spicy sauce hits the spot with less fuss. These flavor-packed little sammies are great for entertaining a crowd at brunch, alongside other dishes, or served solo as a stand-alone lunch (in which case you should allot two per person).

MAKE THE SLAW: In a medium bowl, whisk together the mayonnaise, mustard, vinegar, celery seed, and salt and pepper to taste. Add the cabbage and carrot and toss to coat. Set aside. (The slaw can be made up to 24 hours in advance and stored, tightly covered, in the fridge.)

Remove the cooked chicken breasts from the bag, discard any liquid, and thoroughly pat the chicken dry with paper towels.

Melt the butter in a large skillet or sauté pan over medium heat until it sizzles and begins to brown. Add the chicken breasts in a single layer and cook until the first side is golden brown, 2 to 3 minutes. Flip the breasts and cook to brown the other side, 1 to 2 minutes more. If you're using chicken that has come directly from the refrigerator, flip the breasts again and cook for an additional 2 to 3 minutes to ensure that they're heated through.

Transfer the chicken to a cutting board. Slice each chicken breast in half at an angle to create 2 pieces of approximately equal size. Set aside.

Add the garlic to the pan and cook over medium heat, stirring constantly, until fragrant, about 30 seconds, then immediately add the honey and hot sauce. Let the mixture come to a simmer, stir to combine it, and cook until the mixture is thick enough to coat the back of a spoon, about 1 minute. Add the reserved chicken to the pan, add the thyme, heat for 30 seconds in the sauce, then flip to coat the other side. Remove the pan from the heat.

Divide the slaw between the bottom halves of each biscuit, followed by a piece of chicken breast. Spoon any additional sauce evenly over each piece of chicken, then close the sandwiches by placing the biscuit tops on each.

BAKED CHICKEN PARMESAN

Chicken parm is a cherished mainstay of Italian-American cooking. I confess I adore the classic version, but I often don't have the time or energy required to go through the steps of breading and frying the chicken before the dish can be assembled. My goal for this version was to make the recipe faster, easier, and healthier without sacrificing the homey, comforting quality of the original. To make this dish even simpler to throw together on short notice, the marinara can be made in advance, chilled, and stored in an airtight container in your refrigerator for up to 2 weeks—or (and don't tell anyone) I even give you my blessing to use your favorite store-bought tomato sauce. Serve it with crusty bread, plain rice, or buttered pasta.

Preheat the oven to 425°F.

MAKE THE MARINARA: Heat 3 tablespoons of the olive oil in a medium saucepan over medium heat until it shimmers. Add the garlic to the pot and cook, stirring constantly, until it's very fragrant and begins to turn light golden brown, 1 to 2 minutes. Stir in the pepper flakes to taste and the thyme, followed immediately by 1½ cups of the cherry tomatoes and a pinch of salt. Cook for 2 to 3 minutes, stirring occasionally until the tomatoes have released their liquid, softened, and are beginning to lose their shape. Add the crushed tomatoes and stir to combine. Let the mixture come to a boil, and then lower the heat to a simmer and cook, stirring occasionally, for about 8 minutes, until slightly thickened and reduced. Remove the sauce from the heat, season to taste with salt and black pepper, then stir in the ¼ cup of basil.

Remove the cooked chicken breasts from the bag, discard any liquid, and thoroughly pat them dry with paper towels. Pour the marinara into a 9 by 13-inch baking dish or casserole, and then lay the breasts into the sauce, smooth side up, so that the sauce comes about halfway up each breast.

In a small bowl, toss the bread crumbs with the Parmesan, the remaining 1 tablespoon of olive oil, and a pinch of salt.

Divide the mozzarella so that there's a roughly even layer covering the surface of each chicken breast. Sprinkle the bread crumb mixture evenly over the mozzarella (don't worry if some of the cheese or bread crumbs fall into the surrounding sauce).

Transfer the pan to the oven and bake until the cheese and bread crumbs have turned golden brown and the marinara is bubbling, 20 to 25 minutes.

Remove from the oven and sprinkle with the remaining ½ cup of cherry tomatoes and additional torn basil. Serve family style or transfer the chicken to individual plates and spoon the extra marinara from the pan on top.

SERVES 4

🕐 **45 MINUTES**

MARINARA

4 tablespoons extra-virgin olive oil

3 cloves garlic, thinly sliced

Pinch of red pepper flakes

½ teaspoon fresh, or ⅛ teaspoon dried, thyme or oregano leaves

1 pint (2 cups) cherry tomatoes, halved, ½ cup reserved for garnish

Salt

1 (14-ounce) can crushed tomatoes (preferably San Marzano)

¼ cup loosely packed basil leaves, torn, plus more for garnish

Freshly ground black pepper

1 **MASTER RECIPE** Chicken Breast (page 42), just cooked or straight from the fridge

⅓ cup coarse unseasoned bread crumbs (preferably panko)

⅓ cup (about 1½ ounce) grated Parmesan (preferably Parmigiano-Reggiano)

8 ounces fresh mozzarella, sliced ¼ inch thick

CHICKEN SALAD
WITH CARROT GINGER DRESSING

SERVES 4
🕐 **10 MINUTES**

CARROT GINGER DRESSING

1 tablespoon honey

1 tablespoon Sriracha

2 tablespoons soy sauce

¼ cup rice vinegar

2 green onions, coarsely chopped, thinly sliced dark green parts reserved for garnish

2 carrots, peeled and sliced ¼ inch thick, about 2 cups

1 tablespoon peeled, thinly sliced against the grain fresh ginger, from about 1 (1-inch) piece

½ cup canola or other neutral vegetable oil

2 teaspoons toasted sesame oil

Salt and freshly ground black pepper

2 heads prewashed romaine lettuce, halved and sliced across into 1-inch pieces, stem ends and cores discarded

½ daikon, or a handful of red radishes, thinly sliced (about 1 cup)

1 MASTER RECIPE Chicken Breast (page 42), just cooked or straight from the fridge

2 tablespoons toasted sesame seeds, for garnish

My inspiration for this dish will be familiar to anyone who frequents Japanese steak houses (aka teppanyaki) in America. Typically this salad is served as a starter before meatier dishes, but I think the zingy carrot ginger dressing is appealing enough to warrant a more substantial treatment. To make this a complete meal, I add tender chicken breast (great warm or straight from the fridge) as a foil for the tangy dressing and crunchy lettuce, making it perfect for lunch or a light dinner. This dressing makes more than you'll likely need for one batch of salad, but it will keep perfectly well in your refrigerator for up to 2 weeks.

MAKE THE DRESSING: Add the honey, Sriracha, soy sauce, vinegar, green onions (white and light green parts only), carrots, and ginger to the bowl of a blender or food processor, and pulse until you've created a coarse puree. With the blender running on low speed, pour in the canola and sesame oils in a thin stream to emulsify. Season to taste with salt and black pepper.

Place the lettuce and daikon in a large bowl and toss with half the dressing to coat—add more to taste. Any leftover dressing can be stored in an airtight container for up to 2 weeks, for another use.

Remove the cooked chicken breasts from the bag, discard any liquid, and thoroughly pat them dry with paper towels. The chicken is perfect to eat as is, but if you want to serve it slightly warm, add the breasts to a lightly greased grill pan or cast-iron skillet. Cook over medium-high heat for 1 to 2 minutes on each side until golden or grill marks form, adding another 1 to 2 minutes if you want the chicken completely warmed through. Slice each breast into ½-inch pieces against the grain.

Arrange the sliced chicken on the dressed salad, sprinkle with the sesame seeds and reserved green onions, and serve.

2 pounds skinless, boneless
chicken thighs, trimmed of
excess fat (about 8)

Salt

CHICKEN THIGH

For my money, chicken thighs offer one of the best cost-to-flavor ratios of any protein, which helps explain why I almost always have some cooked (sous vide, of course) in my fridge. In fact, the idea for this book sprung in part from chicken thighs' ready adaptability to different dishes and cuisines—they are culinary chameleons! Although bone-in chicken thighs are touted for being juicier and more flavorful than their boneless counterparts, I prefer the latter when cooking sous vide because the technique results in moist, tasty chicken that cooks in half the time. Plus it requires less work to cut or shred the cooked chicken when incorporating it into spin-off dishes such as pot pie or noodle soup.

Preheat the water bath to 65°C (149°F).

Season the chicken thighs with salt and place in a 1-gallon freezer-safe ziplock bag or a vacuum seal bag. Arrange the thighs in a single layer with as little overlap as possible to ensure even cooking. Seal the bag using either the water displacement method (page 12) or a vacuum sealer.

When the water reaches the target temperature, lower the bagged chicken in the water bath (making sure the bag is fully submerged) and cook for 1½ hours (or up to 6 hours), or 2 hours (or up to 7 hours) for bone-in thighs.

Remove the bag from the water bath, transfer it to an ice water bath (see page 18), and chill until completely cold, about 20 minutes. Once cooked and chilled, the chicken can be refrigerated in the bag for up to 10 days.

Alternatively, if you plan on using the just-cooked chicken in a spin-off recipe right away, let it rest in the bag at room temperature for at least 10 minutes or up to 1 hour before proceeding.

COOKING TIP

Don't be alarmed if the cooking juices that collect at the bottom of your cooking bag are still slightly pink. As I discussed in the Chicken Breast master (page 42), the proteins won't fully denature at the slightly lower temperature, but the chicken is perfectly safe.

ADDITIONAL SPIN-OFF IDEAS

Left whole, sous vide chicken thighs are perfect for grilling, dusted with a dry rub or brushed with a barbecue sauce, or breaded and deep fried. Because the chicken is already cooked through, all that is required is a quick dip in hot oil to get a crispy crust without worrying about undercooking. You can also shred the meat and use it as a filling for your favorite enchilada or tamale.

CHICKEN POT PIE

SERVES 4

🕐 1 HOUR

1 MASTER RECIPE Chicken Thigh (page 50), just cooked or straight from the fridge

4 tablespoons unsalted butter

1 onion, cut into ¼-inch dice

1 carrot, peeled and cut into ¼-inch dice

1 celery root or parsnip, peeled and coarsely grated (about 1½ firmly packed cups)

2 cloves garlic, minced

Salt

¼ cup all-purpose flour

1 cup dry sherry or white wine

1 cup chicken stock, homemade (page 176) or store-bought

1 cup heavy cream or crème fraîche

1 cup peas, shelled, fresh or frozen

1 teaspoon fresh thyme leaves

2 teaspoons Worcestershire sauce

½ teaspoon Old Bay seasoning (optional)

Freshly ground white or black pepper

1 (14-oz) package frozen puff pastry, thawed (see Shopping Tip, facing page)

1 large egg, beaten

Flaky sea salt, such as Maldon or fleur de sel

With a flaky crust encasing a rich, creamy filling of chicken and vegetables, pot pie is a wonderfully homey, satisfying dish—even the name conjures up an image of wholesome domesticity. My version hews pretty closely to the classic, but the addition of grated celery root or parsnip is my way of adding more substance to the dish without compromising its creamy richness. My other trick for pot pie greatness is using store-bought puff pastry for the crust, which produces the most ethereally crisp results imaginable with minimal fuss.

Preheat the oven to 400°F. Line a baking sheet with parchment paper.

Remove the cooked chicken thighs from the bag, reserving any liquid in the bag. (If the chicken has been refrigerated for a while, the liquid will have gelled.) Thoroughly pat the chicken dry with paper towels. Cut the chicken into bite-size pieces. Set aside.

Melt the butter in a large Dutch oven or wide-bottomed pot over medium-low heat. Add the onion, carrot, celery root, and garlic. Season with a pinch of salt and cook, stirring frequently, until the vegetables are translucent and softened, 8 to 10 minutes. Do not allow the mixture to brown.

Stir in the flour and cook for 1 minute, then pour in the sherry, stirring constantly. Once the sherry has come to a boil, let it cook for 1 minute, continuing to stir. Stir in the chicken stock, reserved chicken cooking juices, and cream and return to a boil. Lower the heat to a simmer and cook, stirring often, until the mixture is thickened and slightly reduced, another 4 to 5 minutes. Stir in the peas and remove from the heat. Add the thyme, Worcestershire, Old Bay, and chicken thighs and season to taste with salt and pepper.

Divide the filling mixture between 4 (16-ounce) heatproof ramekins or other heatproof baking dishes, such as soufflé dishes. Cut the puff pastry into 4 equal pieces, then place 1 piece over the top of each ramekin so that they're completely covered, with the pastry hanging over the sides. (You may need to roll out the puff pastry on a floured surface first, in order to cover the ramekins completely.) Trim off the excess pastry with a paring knife or kitchen shears, if desired. (I happen to like the rustic look of pastry hanging over the dish—plus the more crust, the better, if you ask me.)

Transfer the pot pies to the prepared baking sheet. Brush the top of each with the beaten egg, sprinkle with flaky salt, and cut a slit in the center of the pastry to allow steam to escape while baking.

Place the pot pies on the middle rack of the oven and bake until the pastry is deep golden brown, 25 to 30 minutes. Remove from the oven and let rest for at least 5 minutes before serving—watch out, they're hot!

My preferred brand of frozen puff pastry is Dufour (made with butter), as opposed to Pepperidge Farm (made with hydrogenated vegetable oil). I think the flavor and texture of the all-butter version are superior, but the alternative is less expensive and more widely available (Dufour is available nationwide at Whole Foods). Either will work for this recipe, but be aware that Dufour comes in a 14-ounce package of 1 sheet, whereas the Pepperidge Farm comes in a 17-ounce package of 2 sheets, so expect to have some excess if using the larger size.

CHICKEN NOODLE SOUP

Folklore would have it that homemade chicken soup is a powerful talisman against sickness, both physical and existential. I won't make such bold claims, but I can certify that mine manages to bring almost all the goodness of the traditional slow-cooked versions in a fraction of the time, even if you use store-bought stock. Of course, if you should happen to have some homemade stock on hand, all the better. Crusty bread or crackers wouldn't hurt, either.

Remove the cooked chicken thighs from the bag, reserving any liquid in the bag. (If the chicken has been refrigerated for a while, the liquid will have gelled.) Thoroughly pat the chicken dry with paper towels.

Heat the olive oil in a large Dutch oven or stockpot over medium-high heat. Add the chicken and brown on both sides until golden, about 2 minutes per side, working in batches if necessary. Remove the browned chicken pieces from the pan and set aside.

Add the onions to the pan and cook, stirring frequently, until softened and deep golden brown in places, about 5 minutes. Add the butter to the pan, stir in the garlic, celery, and carrots, and cook for 1 minute more.

Add the chicken stock and reserved chicken cooking juices to the pot, bring the mixture to a boil, and then lower the heat to a simmer. Using a deep spoon or ladle, skim off any scum that rises to the surface and discard.

While the stock is coming to a boil, shred the chicken into bite-size pieces.

Once the stock is simmering, stir in the egg noodles and continue to simmer until the noodles and vegetables are tender but not falling apart, about 10 minutes. Add the shredded chicken, along with any collected juices, to the pot. Remove the pot from the heat and season to taste with salt, pepper, and hot sauce. Stir in the lemon juice and herbs, ladle into serving bowls, and serve immediately.

SERVES 4 TO 6 GENEROUSLY
🕐 **25 MINUTES**

1 MASTER RECIPE Chicken Thigh (page 50), just cooked or straight from the fridge

1 tablespoon olive oil

1 yellow onion, cut into ½-inch dice

1 tablespoon unsalted butter

3 cloves garlic, minced

2 celery stalks, sliced ½ inch thick

2 carrots, peeled and sliced ¼ inch thick

2 quarts chicken stock, homemade (page 176) or low-sodium store-bought broth

4 ounces wide egg noodles (about 2 cups)

Salt and freshly ground white or black pepper

Hot sauce (optional)

1 tablespoon freshly squeezed lemon juice

3 tablespoons chopped parsley, dill, or celery leaf, or a mixture

PALEO CHICKEN STIR-FRY
WITH PINEAPPLE AND RED PEPPER

SERVES 4
🕐 **20 MINUTES**

1 MASTER RECIPE Chicken Thigh (page 50), just cooked or straight from the fridge

4 tablespoons coconut aminos, or 2 tablespoons low-sodium soy sauce

3 tablespoons coconut oil

1 red bell pepper, cut into ¼-inch strips

½ pineapple, peeled, cored, and cut into bite-size chunks

1 tablespoon peeled, minced fresh ginger, from about 1 (1-inch) piece

3 cloves garlic, minced

1 bunch green onions, white and light green parts, thinly sliced, dark green parts reserved for garnish

1 serrano or jalapeño chile, thinly sliced, seeded if desired

1 teaspoon ground allspice

1 teaspoon freshly ground black pepper

1 tablespoon coconut vinegar or apple cider vinegar

Salt

In a book about adapting sous vide to modern lifestyles, I'd be remiss if I didn't include at least one recipe geared toward the Paleo diet. After all, a great many devotees of the sous vide method use it in part because it facilitates a diet that's high in protein and low in carbohydrates. With that in mind, the combination of sweet pineapple and peppers with punchy aromatics like ginger, chiles, and allspice is sure to please any palate, regardless of diet. Note that because legumes like soy are a no-no for the Paleo diet, I opt for coconut aminos, derived from the fermented sap of coconut palms—but if you're not strictly following the diet, you can sub soy sauce. Seasoning with additional salt is optional here; feel free to omit it.

Remove the cooked chicken thighs from the bag, reserving any liquid in the bag. (If the chicken has been refrigerated for a while, the liquid will have gelled.) Thoroughly pat the chicken dry with paper towels.

Slice the chicken against the grain into ½-inch-thick strips. Place in a bowl and toss with 2 tablespoons of the coconut aminos (or 1 tablespoon of the soy sauce).

Heat 1 tablespoon of the coconut oil in a large wok or large skillet over high heat until shimmering and giving off wisps of smoke, and then add the chicken. Stir-fry the chicken, tossing and stirring occasionally, until the edges begin to brown, 2 to 3 minutes. Remove the wok from the heat and transfer the chicken to a large bowl. Set aside.

Return the wok to the heat, add another 1 tablespoon of the coconut oil, and heat until shimmering and giving off wisps of smoke. Add the bell pepper and pineapple and stir-fry until the pepper is charred in places and beginning to soften, 2 to 3 minutes. Transfer mixture to the bowl containing the chicken.

Return the wok to the heat, add the remaining 1 tablespoon of coconut oil, and heat until shimmering and giving off wisps of smoke. Add the ginger, garlic, green onions (white and light green parts only), and chile and cook, stirring constantly, until aromatic and beginning to brown, about 1 minute.

Add the reserved chicken and vegetable mixture along with any juices that have collected in the bowl, the remaining 2 tablespoons of coconut aminos (or 1 tablespoon of soy sauce), allspice, black pepper, coconut vinegar, and reserved cooking juices to the wok. Toss the mixture together and cook for 1 minute more. Season to taste with salt, if desired.

Transfer the stir-fry to bowls, garnish with the reserved green onions, and serve immediately.

PORK

2 pounds pork tenderloin or boneless pork loin (also sold as boneless chops) cut into 4 (¾- to 1½-inch-thick) pieces, or 4 (¾- to 1½-inch-thick) bone-in pork chops (about 3 pounds)

Salt

QUICK-COOKED PORK

There's no way to hide my love of pork, particularly the loin cuts, which are the leanest and most delicate. Like chicken, "the other white meat" has enormous culinary versatility but is easily overcooked using conventional cooking methods, making it particularly well suited to sous vide's gentle heat.

Made up of the meat around a pig's ribs, the loin is comprised of two sections: the larger loin muscle, which makes up the pork chop, and the much smaller tenderloin that runs alongside it. These cuts perform differently, which is why I've recommended specific cuts in the following spin-off recipes. Kept whole, the delicate tenderloin makes an elegant roast topped with a lemony piccata sauce, while the larger loin can be either left on the bone for juicy thick-cut pork chops served with your favorite applesauce (or better still—my Indian-spice chutney), or sliced off the bone and added to a stir-fry or skewered into kebabs.

Preheat the water bath to 58°C (136.4°F).

Season the pork with salt and place in a 1-gallon freezer-safe ziplock bag or a vacuum seal bag. Arrange the pieces in a single layer with as little overlap as possible to ensure even cooking. Seal the bag using either the water displacement method (page 12) or a vacuum sealer.

When the water reaches the target temperature, lower the bagged pork in the water bath (making sure the bag is fully submerged) and cook for 90 minutes (or up to 5 hours).

Remove the bag from the water bath, transfer it to an ice water bath (see page 18), and chill until completely cold, about 10 minutes. Once cooked and chilled, the pork can be refrigerated in the bag for up to 1 week.

Alternatively, if you plan on using the just-cooked pork in a spin-off recipe right away, let it rest in the bag at room temperature for at least 10 minutes or up to 1 hour before proceeding.

SHOPPING TIP

The recipes in this section call for pork chop (pork loin) and tenderloin, but be sure not to confuse the two cuts; some grocery stores will often mislabel boneless pork loin as tenderloin. Even at its largest, a whole tenderloin will weigh no more than 1 pound or so, whereas a whole loin is more in the neighborhood of 8 to 10 pounds. Both can be cooked at the same temperature for the same duration, which is why I've bundled them into this one master recipe.

COOKING TIP

The pork in this dish is cooked medium rare, with a pink interior, which is my preferred doneness. It's perfectly safe to eat pork this way, but if the pink color makes you uncomfortable, just raise the water bath temperature to 60°C (140°F) and cook for the same amount of time, and you'll still end up with very moist meat.

ADDITIONAL SPIN-OFF IDEAS

Whether you're cooking boneless loin, chops, or tenderloin, this time and temperature will make the most of your pork loin cuts. Bread and fry bone-in loin to make the juiciest Southern fried chops, coat boneless loin with a char sui marinade and broil until just caramelized, or use your favorite rub to make the best barbecue tenderloin.

PORK TENDERLOIN PICCATA

SERVES 4

🕐 **20 MINUTES**

1 MASTER RECIPE Quick-Cooked Pork (page 60; made with tenderloin, 2 to 4 pieces, depending on their size), just cooked or straight from the fridge

1 tablespoon all-purpose flour

2 tablespoons olive oil

4 tablespoons unsalted butter

PICCATA SAUCE

3 cloves garlic, thinly sliced

2 shallots, thinly sliced

Generous pinch of red pepper flakes

¾ cup dry white wine

1½ cups chicken stock, homemade (page 176) or low-sodium store-bought broth

1½ tablespoons capers, drained and coarsely chopped

1 teaspoon fresh thyme leaves, coarsely chopped

¼ cup chopped fresh Italian parsley

1 teaspoon Dijon mustard

1 tablespoon freshly squeezed lemon juice

Salt and freshly ground black pepper

Piccata is a classic Italian preparation that has largely fallen out of favor in recent years, but I think it's high time to bring it back. Topped with a lively sauce featuring butter, capers, herbs, and lemon, it's undeniably delicious. Whether served over chicken, veal, or, as I've done here, lean pork tenderloin, luscious lemony piccata is a simple yet elegant meal that's easy to pull off for a midweek meal. Roasted vegetables, potatoes, or rice round it out nicely.

Remove the cooked pork tenderloins from the bag, discarding any liquid. Thoroughly pat the pork dry with paper towels. If you are using 2 larger tenderloins, cut them in half so that you have 4 pieces. Dust evenly with flour to coat.

Heat the olive oil in a large skillet or sauté pan over medium-high heat until shimmering. Swirl in 2 tablespoons of the butter (which should immediately sizzle) and cook until golden brown.

Place the tenderloins in the pan and sear on the underside until deep golden brown, about 1 minute, and then roll them a quarter turn and sear for 1 minute more. Continue to sear and roll each tenderloin until all sides are browned, 4 to 6 minutes total. If you've taken the tenderloin straight from the fridge, add an additional 2 or 3 minutes to ensure they're heated through. Transfer the tenderloins to a platter and cover loosely with aluminum foil. Set aside.

MAKE THE PICCATA SAUCE: Lower the heat to medium, add the garlic and shallots, and cook 1 to 2 minutes, until beginning to brown. Stir in the red pepper flakes, followed by the white wine, and bring the mixture to a boil, scraping the pan with a wooden spoon to deglaze; cook for 2 minutes, until reduced by about half. Add the chicken stock and capers, then return the mixture to a boil and cook until again reduced by half, 3 to 5 minutes. Remove from the heat and whisk in the thyme, parsley, mustard, and lemon juice, followed by the remaining 2 tablespoons of butter. Season to taste with salt and pepper.

Slice the pork tenderloin into ¼-inch-thick medallions, transfer back to the platter, and pour the sauce on top.

GRILLED PORK CHOPS
WITH APPLE CHUTNEY

Serving pork chops with applesauce may be pure Americana, but this recipe breathes new life into this pairing by swapping out the plain ol' applesauce for an Indian-inspired apple chutney. The chutney's lively balance of sweet, sour, and spice adds a layer of complexity, making a sophisticated foil for the rich, savory pork. It's delicious warm, spooned over the pork, but the chutney can also be made in advance and served either cold or at room temperature.

MAKE THE CHUTNEY: Heat the oil over medium-high heat until shimmering. Add the shallots and ginger and cook, stirring occasionally, until they begin to brown, about 5 minutes. Stir in the mustard seeds (they'll make a popping noise), raisins, and chiles and cook for 1 to 2 minutes, until the raisins begin to puff and color. Stir in the apple, a pinch of salt, and ¾ teaspoon of the garam masala and cook for 1 minute. Reduce the heat to medium and stir in the vinegar and ¼ cup of the brown sugar. Cover the pot and cook, stirring occasionally, until the apple has softened and begun to lose its shape, 10 to 12 minutes. Remove from the heat, stir in the thyme and lime juice, and season to taste with additional salt. Set aside or let cool before transferring to an airtight container and refrigerate for up to 2 weeks.

Remove the cooked pork chops from the bag, discarding any liquid in the bag. (If the chops have been refrigerated for a while, the liquid may have gelled.) Thoroughly pat the pork dry with paper towels.

Combine the remaining ¾ teaspoon of garam masala and 1 tablespoon of brown sugar in a small bowl. Rub the spice mixture evenly over the pork chops to coat.

Heat a grill pan or skillet over medium-high heat. Once the pan is hot, use a paper towel and a little additional oil to grease the pan and prevent sticking. Add the pork chops to the hot pan and grill for 4 minutes, flipping them after each minute, for a total of 3 flips, cooking in batches if necessary. If you're cooking the pork chops straight from the fridge, double the cooking time, cooking for a total of 8 minutes, flipping every 2 minutes. (Note: If you want nice cross-hatch grill marks, rotate the chops 45° after the second flip.)

Transfer the pork chops to individual plates. Or, if you are serving more than 4 people, transfer the chops to a cutting board instead and allow them to rest for 5 minutes; then cut the meat off the bone, slice it in a slight diagonal against the grain, and divide the slices among the plates. Top the pork with a generous spoonful of chutney and garnish with the cilantro and lime wedges.

SERVES 4 TO 6
🕐 **30 MINUTES**

APPLE CHUTNEY

2 tablespoons canola or other neutral vegetable oil, plus more for the pan

2 shallots, minced (about ¼ cup)

1 tablespoon peeled, minced fresh ginger, from about 1 (1-inch) piece

1 tablespoon whole brown mustard seed or cracked yellow mustard seed

¼ cup golden raisins

2 serrano or jalapeño chiles, halved, seeded if desired, and thinly sliced

4 Granny Smith apples, peeled, cored, and cut into ½-inch dice

Pinch salt

1½ teaspoons garam masala

2 tablespoons apple cider vinegar

¼ cup firmly packed light brown sugar, plus 1 tablespoon for coating the pork

2 teaspoons fresh thyme leaves, coarsely chopped

2 tablespoons fresh lime juice

1 MASTER RECIPE Quick-Cooked Pork (page 60; made with bone-in pork chops), just cooked or straight from the fridge

¼ cup cilantro, coarsely chopped, for garnish

4 lime wedges, for garnish

DRUNKEN NOODLES

SERVES 4 TO 6

🕐 **15 MINUTES**

1 MASTER RECIPE Quick-Cooked Pork (page 60; made with boneless loin pieces), just cooked or straight from the fridge

14 to 16 ounces dried wide rice noodles

SAUCE

2 tablespoons light brown sugar

2 tablespoons fish sauce

¼ cup oyster sauce, or 2 tablespoons additional fish sauce

¼ cup soy sauce

¼ cup sweet soy sauce, or 2 tablespoons additional brown sugar and 3 tablespoons additional soy sauce

1 teaspoon freshly ground white pepper

3 tablespoons canola or other neutral vegetable oil

3 cloves garlic, thinly sliced

2 shallots, thinly sliced (about ½ cup)

2 to 4 red Thai or other fresh red chiles, such as Fresno or finger, thinly sliced (depending on your heat preference)

3 or 4 green onions, halved lengthwise through the bulb end, then cut into 1-inch lengths (about 1½ cups)

1 red bell pepper, cut into ¼-inch strips

1 cup Thai basil leaves, loosely packed

Various explanations exist for the name of this popular Thai dish. Some say that its spicy, sweet flavors make it the perfect food to accompany drinking—or to recover the morning after. Others say that the wide assortment of typical additions—sliced tomato, baby corn, Chinese cabbage, button mushrooms, eggs, and tofu—seems to have been thrown together by someone in a state of inebriation. Whatever the origin of the name, this is a dish I crave no matter my state of sobriety. Feel free to add in any of the additions I mentioned above, or others of your own choosing.

Remove the cooked pork loin pieces from the bag, discarding any liquid in the bag. (If the pork has been refrigerated for a while, the liquid may have gelled.) Thoroughly pat the pork dry with paper towels. Set aside.

Cook the rice noodles in a large pot of water for 2 minutes, until tender but with a slight bite, stirring frequently to prevent sticking. Drain and rinse with cold water. Alternatively, soak the noodles in a bowl filled with hot tap water for 30 minutes, and then drain and rinse with cold water. Set aside.

PREPARE THE SAUCE: Mix together the brown sugar, fish sauce, oyster sauce, soy sauce, sweet soy sauce, and white pepper. Lightly brush the pork loin pieces on both sides with the sauce to coat. Reserve the rest of the sauce for later.

In a large skillet or wok, heat 1 tablespoon of the oil over medium-high heat until shimmering. Sear the pork loin pieces for 4 minutes, flipping them after each minute, for a total of three flips, until deeply browned, almost blackened. Turn off the heat, transfer the pork to a cutting board, and slice it crosswise into ¼-inch strips. Set aside.

Return the skillet or wok to medium-high heat, add the remaining 2 tablespoons of oil, and heat until shimmering. Add the garlic, shallot, and chiles and cook for 30 seconds. Add the green onion and bell pepper and cook, stirring frequently, until they begin to brown and soften, 3 to 5 minutes. Add the reserved sauce and cooked noodles and cook, stirring frequently, until the noodles have absorbed the sauce and softened, about 4 minutes. Add the sliced pork, along with any juices that have accumulated, and cook for 1 minute more, still stirring. Remove from the heat.

Toss the noodles with the basil, mixing just until the leaves are wilted. Serve immediately.

SOUS VIDE COOKING TIME
15 hours (or up to 20 hours)

2 pounds boneless pork belly;
3 pounds boneless pork shoulder,
skin removed (no more than
4 inches thick); or 4 pounds
pork ribs

Salt

SLOW-COOKED PORK

Succulent, *juicy*, and *unctuous* aren't just some of my favorite lascivious-sounding food words—they also explain why slow-cooked sous vide pork will always hold a central place in my gastronomic affections. For this master recipe, take note that even though the spin-offs call for different cuts, the cooking time and temperature work the same for each. For both the belly and shoulder, make sure the cuts are boneless and the skin is removed. For the ribs, make sure to use either St. Louis–style or baby back ribs, which are both trimmed from the larger rib cut. Because excess bone is removed, these two have a higher percentage of meat and will fit better in the cooking bags.

Because this master recipe requires longer—albeit hands-off—cooking time, and also because it makes excellent leftovers, I call for cooking a larger amount. Chances are you'll want to prepare a big batch of sticky BBQ baby back ribs or falling-apart carnitas tacos for a large crowd anyway. See the Braised Beef Batch Cooking tip (page 87) for info on storing and reheating leftovers.

Preheat the water bath to 75°C (167°F).

Season the pork with salt and place in a 1-gallon freezer-safe ziplock bag or a vacuum seal bag. In the case of ribs, it's okay if the racks overlap somewhat because of the extended cooking time. Seal the bag using either the water displacement method (page 12) or a vacuum sealer.

When the water reaches the target temperature, lower the bagged pork in the water bath (making sure the bag is fully submerged) and cook for 15 hours (or up to 20 hours). I recommend covering the bath with plastic wrap or aluminum foil to minimize evaporation (see page 16 for explanation) and ensure that the bag remains fully submerged the entire time.

Remove the bag from the water bath, transfer it to an ice water bath (see page 18), and chill until completely cold, about 30 minutes. Once cooked and chilled, the pork can be refrigerated in the bag for up to 1 week.

Alternatively, if you plan on using the just-cooked pork in a spin-off recipe right away, let it rest in the bag at room temperature for at least 20 minutes or up to 1 hour, and then skim off the excess fat (see Storing Tip, facing page) before proceeding.

COOKING TIP

The high fat and high moisture found in pork belly and shoulder make them even more prone to sizzling and sputtering than bacon, so I strongly recommend investing in a splatter guard (a round, fine-mesh screen) to cover the pan while you cook. This allows the moisture to evaporate while the meat cooks, but prevents any risk of your being hit by projectiles of hot fat. Splatter guards cost as little as ten dollars, and they're useful for anything that spatters, from bubbling tomato sauce to hot frying oil.

STORING TIP

I recommend you save the juices that get released during the cooking process; they add a wonderful richness to sauces. You'll need to skim off the excess fat, which can also be saved to cook and used as you would residual bacon grease. To do this, while the cooking bag is still hot, pour the liquid into a measuring cup. The fat will rise to the top, and you can skim it off with a ladle or spoon. The fat can also (and more easily) be removed with a slotted spoon or a coarse strainer after it's been refrigerated. If you're left with an ample amount of fat, I also recommend reserving it for another use—or, in the case of the Carnitas Tacos with Salsa Verde (page 73), using it in the same recipe. Before storing, heat the excess fat over medium-low heat in a small saucepan until it begins to boil and then continue to cook it until no moisture remains, at which point it will cease sizzling and bubbling. Both the clarified cooking juices and solidified fat can be stored in an airtight container for up to 2 weeks in the fridge or 6 months in the freezer.

ADDITIONAL SPIN-OFF IDEAS

Use this method anytime you want tender, fall-apart pork. For shoulder, shred and douse with any style of barbecue sauce to make pulled pork sandwiches, or stir it into hearty stews like pozole. Use pork belly to make luscious Chinese steamed buns, slathered with hoisin, or anywhere you would use bacon.

PORK BELLY BLT

SERVES 4

🕐 **15 MINUTES**

1 MASTER RECIPE Slow-Cooked Pork (page 68; made with skinless pork belly), just cooked or straight from the fridge

HERBED AIOLI

1 clove garlic, finely crushed or minced

Pinch salt

1 teaspoon freshly squeezed lime or lemon juice

½ cup mayonnaise, homemade (page 172) or store-bought

1 tablespoon grainy mustard

½ teaspoon smoked paprika

1 tablespoon chopped fresh dill, basil, or tarragon

Freshly ground black pepper

1 teaspoon canola or other neutral vegetable oil

8 slices hearty sandwich bread, such as sourdough or whole wheat (toasted if desired)

4 to 8 large romaine lettuce leaves, washed, cut in half as necessary to fit your bread

1 or 2 large beefsteak tomatoes (preferably heirloom), cored and cut into ¼-inch-thick slices (4 to 8 slices total, enough to cover 4 slices of bread)

While I admit that pork belly might be a bit too rich to qualify for most people's idea of an everyday dish, once you taste how satisfying this crispy, tender meat is, you might find that it becomes a constant craving. Once you have the belly cooked sous vide, this sandwich takes no longer to throw together than your average BLT—but I can promise you the results are anything but average. Ideally, serve with potato salad or chips.

Remove the cooked pork belly from the bag, either discarding any liquid in the bag or saving the cooking juices for another use (see Storing Tip on page 69). (If the pork has been refrigerated for a while, the liquid will have gelled.) Thoroughly pat dry with paper towels, then slice into ¼- to ½-inch-thick pieces. You should end up with 8 to 16 pieces total.

PREPARE THE AIOLI: Mix the garlic, a pinch of salt, and lime juice in a bowl, then stir in the mayonnaise, mustard, paprika, and dill. Season to taste with black pepper and additional salt.

Line a sheet tray or platter with paper towels and set aside.

Heat the oil in a large skillet (preferably cast-iron) or sauté pan over medium-high heat until shimmering. Carefully place the pork belly pieces in the pan in a single layer (it's okay if they touch), working in batches if necessary. Cook the pork belly pieces until they've rendered fat, becoming crispy and golden brown, about 5 minutes per side. (I recommend placing a splatter guard over the pan while they cook—see Cooking Tip on page 69.) Transfer the pork belly pieces to the paper towel–lined tray and season lightly with additional salt.

Spread each slice of bread generously with the aioli. Place 1 or 2 pieces of romaine leaves on top of 4 slices of bread (crush the central rib with the heel of your hand to flatten, if needed) to cover completely. Arrange 2 or 3 pieces of seared pork belly evenly on top of the lettuce, then top with 1 or 2 tomato slices. Place the top half of bread on top to close, pressing down lightly so that the sandwich holds together.

CARNITAS TACOS
WITH SALSA VERDE

The mark of great carnitas is the flavorful golden crust that forms as the pork cooks in hot lard. To accomplish that, this recipe calls for using the fat rendered from the pork as it cooks for that final step. Depending on the fattiness of your pork shoulder, you may need to supplement with a little additional fat to have enough—store-bought lard or vegetable oil will work fine. To truly send this pork into the stratosphere, I pair it with a bright and tangy salsa verde—all your wildest taco dreams will come true.

Remove the cooked pork shoulder from the bag, reserving any liquid in the bag. (If the shoulder has been refrigerated for a while, the liquid will have gelled.) Separate the fat from the other liquid (see Storing Tip on page 69) and set both aside. Thoroughly pat the pork shoulder dry with paper towels and then cut into 4 portions of equal thickness.

Line a sheet tray or platter with paper towels and set aside.

Heat the lard in a large Dutch oven or wide-bottomed pot over medium heat until shimmering. (I recommend using a splatter guard to avoid sizzling fat mishaps—see Cooking Tip on page 69.)

Carefully place the shoulder pieces in the pot and cook, flipping the pieces approximately every 5 minutes, until they have turned deep golden brown all over, about 20 to 30 minutes. Transfer the browned pork pieces to the paper towel–lined tray, tent loosely with aluminum foil to keep warm, and set aside.

PREPARE THE SALSA VERDE: Combine the garlic, onion, tomatillos, cilantro, and cumin in a blender and blend into a coarse puree. Set aside.

Drain all but ¼ cup of the fat in the pan (the pork will have rendered more while browning) and discard (or save for another use, such as the next time you make carnitas). Pour in the salsa verde, which should sizzle aggressively when it hits the fat (use that splash guard!). Increase the heat to medium-high and cook for 1 minute. Add the reserved cooking juices to the pan and cook, stirring occasionally, until the mixture has thickened enough to coat the back of a spoon, about 15 minutes. Season to taste with salt and pepper.

While the sauce is reducing, warm the tortillas in a skillet or griddle for about 30 seconds, turning once. Transfer the warm tortillas to a serving plate.

Coarsely chop the pork shoulder and sprinkle with the flaky salt, then transfer to a serving bowl. Arrange the radishes, lime wedges, avocado slices, and chopped cilantro into small bowls (or together on one plate). Set the warmed tortillas out on a plate and transfer the salsa verde to a small bowl. Serve immediately, letting everyone assemble into tacos.

SERVES 6 TO 8
🕐 **50 MINUTES**

1 MASTER RECIPE Slow-Cooked Pork (page 68; made with shoulder), just cooked or straight from the fridge

¼ cup lard or neutral vegetable oil

SALSA VERDE

5 cloves garlic, coarsely chopped

1 small white onion, coarsely chopped

1 pound peeled tomatillos, quartered

½ cup cilantro, coarsely chopped

¾ teaspoon ground cumin

Salt and freshly ground black pepper

18 to 24 corn tortillas

Flaky sea salt, such as Maldon or fleur de sel, for garnish

1 cup sliced radishes, for garnish

6 to 8 lime wedges, from about 2 limes, for garnish

1 avocado, peeled, pitted, and cut into slices, for garnish

½ cup coarsely chopped cilantro, for garnish

BBQ PORK RIBS

SERVES 4

🕐 **35 MINUTES**

1 MASTER RECIPE Slow-Cooked Pork (page 68; made with baby back or St. Louis–style ribs), just cooked or straight from the fridge

SPICE MIX

1 tablespoon paprika

2 teaspoons granulated garlic

1½ teaspoons freshly ground black pepper

1½ teaspoons ground cumin

½ teaspoons cayenne

½ teaspoons dried oregano

BARBECUE SAUCE

1 teaspoon canola oil or lard

1 shallot, thinly sliced

3 canned chipotles in adobo, seeded if desired, chopped

6 ounces stout or other dark beer (½ bottle or can—drink the rest!)

¾ cup ketchup

¼ cup firmly packed dark brown sugar

2 tablespoons cider vinegar

1 tablespoon Dijon or yellow mustard

Barbecue purists may balk at the idea of using sous vide, but these are some of the most succulent, flavorful ribs you'll find outside the realm of a pitmaster. If you don't want to make sauce from scratch, substitute 1½ tablespoons of store-bought chili powder for the spice mix (make sure the mix doesn't contain salt) and use ¾ cup of store-bought barbecue sauce. Combine it with the cooking juices from the pork and reduce until it thickens. Either way, you'll have twice as much as needed; save any extra for the next time you make ribs.

Remove the cooked ribs from the bag, reserving any liquid in the bag and skimming out any fat (see Storing Tip on page 69). (If the ribs have been refrigerated for a while, the liquid will have gelled—if so, use a spoon or fingers to remove the solidified fat.) Thoroughly pat the ribs dry with paper towels.

MAKE THE SPICE MIX: Combine the paprika, granulated garlic, black pepper, cumin, cayenne, and dried oregano in a small bowl.

Season the ribs with 1½ tablespoons of the spice mix, putting most of the seasoning on the meaty (as opposed to bony) side of the ribs. Rub in the spice mix so that it adheres. Set aside.

Preheat the broiler to medium and set the rack 12 inches away from the heat source. Line a baking sheet with parchment paper or aluminum foil and lightly grease with additional oil.

MAKE THE BARBECUE SAUCE: Heat the oil in a small saucepan over medium-high heat until shimmering. Add the shallot and sauté, stirring occasionally, until it softens and begins to brown, 3 to 5 minutes. Stir in the remaining 1½ tablespoons spice mix and the chipotles and cook, stirring constantly, for 1 minute. Add the beer, ketchup, brown sugar, vinegar, and mustard, along with the reserved cooking juices from the pork. Remove the pan from the heat and transfer to a blender or, using an immersion blender, puree the mixture until smooth. Return the pan to medium heat, bring the mixture to a boil, and cook until the liquid has reduced by about half and is thick enough to coat the back of a spoon, about 10 minutes. Set aside.

While the sauce is simmering, transfer the seasoned ribs to the prepared tray and arrange in a single layer, meaty side up. Place under the broiler and cook until the ribs are sizzling and dark brown, 6 to 10 minutes. It's okay if they start to blacken slightly in places but watch it closely, as broilers vary widely in strength. Remove the ribs from the broiler and generously spoon the reduced barbecue sauce on top to cover completely (the remaining sauce can be refrigerated up to 2 weeks). Return the ribs to the broiler and cook until the sauce is sizzling and turned a shade darker, 2 to 3 minutes more. Transfer to a cutting board and cut into individual ribs. Serve immediately.

If you feel the itch to make these ribs a backyard affair, finish them on a grill. Set up your grill for a two-zone fire (also sometimes called indirect heat grilling): If using charcoal, light your coals for a medium-sized fire; once the grills are lit, spread them so that they cover half the bottom grate. If using a gas grill, light half the burners on medium heat, or, if your grill has an upper rack, simply light all the burners. The goal is to have a zone with higher heat for direct grilling and a cooler zone for ambient (oven-like) heat. Use the direct heat to brown the ribs, placing the ribs meat side down, then flip the ribs over and finish them over indirect heat for the final glazing step.

BEEF

---

4 (1- to 1½-inch-thick) boneless steaks (made with the cut of your choice, such as NY strip, rib eye, filet mignon, or skirt steak; about 2½ to 4 pounds)

Salt

1 tablespoon soy sauce (optional)

STEAK

There's no denying that steak is the poster child for sous vide cooking. The iconic image of a thick hunk of steak, sliced to reveal an interior that's an evenly rosy ruby pink from edge to edge is enticing, to say the least. Getting a reliably juicy, beautifully cooked steak every time is a fantastic reason to use sous vide—but it needn't be reserved only for times when you're cooking expensive prime cuts like a gloriously marbled, thick-cut aged rib eye or an ultra-lean filet mignon. The even, gentle heat of sous vide cooking will make the most out of any sort of steak, including everyday, inexpensive cuts such as skirt, hanger, bavette, or sirloin. The time and temperature required for all these cuts are the same, so whether you make my updated version of Steak Diane or whip up a Korean barbecue feast, this master recipe will deliver excellent results. You can use any cut in the following recipes, but bear in mind their size varies widely. The important thing is to buy approximately 2 pounds of meat and, if you're using thinner cuts of meat such as skirt, arrange the meat in a single layer in the bag.

Sous vide offers yet another bonus when it comes to flexibility: its precise nature gives you full control on how "done" your steak is cooked. Personally, I consider 55°C (131°F) the ideal temperature for cooking tender steaks, but one gal's medium rare is another's tartare. If you or your fellow diners prefer meat more done, cook it at 60°C (140°F) for medium and 65°C (149°F) for medium well. (Note that cooking meat below 52.5°C [126.5°F] isn't safe for longer than 2 hours, so if you like your steak on the rarer side, don't leave it in the water bath beyond that.) If you're catering to a range of preferences, cook all the steaks at the lowest temperature, and in the final searing step, add a few extra minutes in the pan to placate the more well-done crowd.

Preheat the water bath to 55°C (131°F).

Season the steaks with salt and soy sauce and place in a 1-gallon freezer-safe ziplock bag or a vacuum seal bag. Arrange the pieces in a single layer with as little overlap as possible to ensure even cooking. Seal the bag using either the water displacement method (page 12) or a vacuum sealer.

When the water reaches the target temperature, lower the bagged steak in the water bath (making sure the bag is fully submerged) and cook for 1 hour (or up to 5 hours).

Remove the bag from the water bath, transfer it to an ice water bath (page 18), and chill until completely cold, about 15 minutes. Once cooked and chilled, the steak can be refrigerated in the bag for up to 1 week.

 Alternatively, if you plan on using the just-cooked steak in a spin-off recipe right away, let it rest in the bag at room temperature for at least 10 minutes or up to 1 hour before proceeding.

COOKING TIP

It's not really necessary to rest your sous vide steaks before slicing since there won't be any carryover cooking time. However, I do think it's helpful to allow the meat to cool slightly if you're going to use it right away in a spin-off dish. This allows time for juices to redistribute and, more importantly, this ensures that the meat won't overcook in the final cooking step.

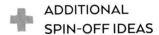

ADDITIONAL SPIN-OFF IDEAS

Serve skirt steak with chimichurri for a riff on the classic Argentinian carne asada, cut a ribeye steak into strips for a fork-and-knife steak salad topped with crumbled blue cheese, or cut a tri-tip into 1-inch cubes to enrich a spicy bean chili.

STEAK
WITH RED WINE MUSTARD SAUCE

SERVES 4
🕐 **15 MINUTES**

1 MASTER RECIPE Steak (page 78; made with the cut of your choice, such as NY strip, rib eye, filet mignon), just cooked or straight from the fridge

1 tablespoon extra-virgin olive oil

3 tablespoons unsalted butter

SAUCE

2 shallots, minced

2 cloves garlic, minced

¼ cup cognac or other brandy or bourbon

½ cup red wine

1 tablespoon Dijon mustard

1 or 2 teaspoons Worcestershire sauce

½ cup heavy cream or crème fraîche

1 or 2 teaspoons freshly squeezed lemon juice

Freshly ground black pepper

2 tablespoons chopped parsley or chives, or a mix

Steak Diane, my inspiration here, was once a common sight in posh restaurants across America, with a tableside preparation capped off by a dramatic flash of flambéed cognac. In spite of its waning popularity, this dish is as delicious as ever, with a sauce that's both piquant and creamy. Traditional recipes call for thinly pounded steaks, which are easy to overcook, but because my version calls for a meltingly tender, already-cooked sous vide steak, there's very little risk of meat drying out during searing. For me, that's the perfect excuse to bring back some old-school cool. Serve it up with mashed potatoes or your favorite side dish to enjoy every last drop of the sauce.

Remove the cooked steak from the bag, reserving any liquid in the bag. Thoroughly pat the steak dry with paper towels. Set aside.

In a cast-iron skillet or sauté pan large enough to hold all your steaks in a single layer (use two pans if necessary), heat the olive oil over high heat until shimmering. Swirl 1 tablespoon of the butter into the pan until it browns and the foam has subsided, 15 to 30 seconds. Carefully place the steaks into the pan, pressing down on the meat with tongs or a spatula for maximum contact with the pan to achieve a nice crust. Cook for 4 to 6 minutes, flipping every 1 minute, until the steaks are deeply golden brown. If the steaks have been just cooked, reduce the searing time to 2 to 3 minutes to avoid overcooking. Transfer the steaks to a platter or tray and cover to keep warm. Set aside.

MAKE THE SAUCE: Discard all but 2 tablespoons of fat in the pan. Return the pan to medium heat. Add the shallots and cook for 2 to 3 minutes, stirring frequently, until translucent and beginning to brown, using a wooden spoon to scrape up any browned bits at the bottom of the pan. Add the garlic and cook 30 seconds to 1 minute more, until aromatic but not browned. Increase heat to high, add the cognac and red wine, bring to a boil, and cook for 1 minute before stirring in the reserved cooking juices, the mustard, 1 teaspoon of the Worcestershire, and the heavy cream. Return the mixture to a boil and cook until it's thick enough to coat the back of a spoon, 2 to 3 minutes. Remove from the heat and stir in the remaining 2 tablespoons of butter, swirling the pan until incorporated. Add the lemon juice, black pepper, and the remaining Worcestershire to taste. Return the steaks to the pan, flipping them to coat with the sauce. Let them sit in the pan for 1 minute to warm slightly.

Transfer the steaks to individual plates, generously spoon the sauce in the pan over each, sprinkle with the parsley or chives, and serve immediately.

For 4 sandwiches, 2 to 2½ pounds of steak makes for generous portions. If you have a larger quantity of steak, you can either reserve it for another use or make more sandwiches.

STEAK SANDWICH
WITH CARAMELIZED ONIONS

I don't think anyone needs to be convinced that caramelized onions are delicious—the sweet, deep onion flavor speaks for itself. However, making true French-style caramelized onions takes time—upwards of 45 minutes. While the traditional approach for caramelization, which calls for sweating the onions over a low flame, can't really be rushed, mine, using higher heat and a little bit of honey to speed up the browning, will give you delicious results in nearly half the time. Paired with a juicy steak and enlivened with a hit of peppery horseradish, it makes for an unbeatable steak sandwich.

Remove the cooked steak from the bag, reserving any liquid in the bag. Thoroughly pat the steak dry with paper towels and trim off any excess gristle or fat.

In a large cast-iron skillet or sauté pan, heat the oil over high heat until shimmering and giving off wisps of smoke. Working in batches if necessary, sear the steaks until nicely browned on both sides, flipping every 1 minute, for a total of 4 to 5 minutes. Transfer the cooked steaks to a platter and set aside.

Allow the pan to continue to heat up until the oil is again giving off wisps of smoke. Add the onions and a generous pinch of salt (which will help the onions soften) and sauté, tossing frequently, until the onions have turned translucent and begun to brown, 3 to 4 minutes. Add butter, garlic, and honey and cook until the butter and honey have begun to brown, 1 to 2 minutes more, before lowering the heat to medium-high. Continue to cook, stirring occasionally, until the onions are completely soft and light golden brown, 15 to 20 minutes more (lower the heat as needed to prevent burning). Stir in the thyme and vinegar and season to taste with salt and pepper.

Return the steaks to the pan, along with the cooking juices, nestling the steaks into the onions so that they are partially covered. Cook for 1 to 2 minutes, until the juices have evaporated and the steaks are warmed. Transfer the steaks to a cutting board and slice them thinly against the grain.

Mix together the mayonnaise, mustard, and 1 tablespoon of the horseradish in a small bowl. Spread the top and bottom layers of each roll with the mayonnaise mixture. Divide the slices of steak among the bottoms of the rolls and then generously spoon the onions over the meat. Sprinkle with the additional horseradish, arugula, and additional thyme and then top with the top bun, pressing down lightly so that the sandwich holds together.

SERVES 4
🕐 **35 MINUTES**

1 MASTER RECIPE Steak (page 78; made with the cut of your choice, such as NY strip, top sirloin, or bavette), just cooked or straight from the fridge

1 tablespoon canola oil

1½ pounds white or yellow onions, thinly sliced (about 2 large onions)

Salt

1 tablespoon unsalted butter

1 clove garlic, minced

2 tablespoons honey

1 teaspoon fresh thyme, chopped, plus more for garnish

1 tablespoon sherry, red wine, or apple cider vinegar

Freshly ground black pepper

¼ cup mayonnaise, homemade (page 172) or store-bought

1 tablespoon grainy mustard (optional)

1 tablespoon horseradish, freshly grated or prepared, plus more for garnish

4 French or other crusty sandwich rolls, halved

1 cup loosely packed arugula, watercress, or other peppery green (optional)

KOREAN BBQ–STYLE STEAK

SERVES 4 TO 6
🕐 **20 MINUTES**

1 MASTER RECIPE Steak (page 78; made with cut of your choice, such as skirt, flap, or sirloin), just cooked or straight from the fridge

MARINADE

½ cup pear nectar, apple juice, or lemon-lime soda, or ¼ cup applesauce

¼ cup soy sauce

2 tablespoons honey or light brown sugar

4 cloves garlic, finely minced or grated

1½ teaspoons peeled and finely minced or grated fresh ginger

3 or 4 green onions, white and light green parts finely chopped, dark green parts thinly sliced and reserved for garnish

1 tablespoon toasted sesame oil

1 teaspoon freshly ground black pepper

1 teaspoon toasted sesame seeds, for garnish

1 large head green leaf lettuce, broken apart into leaves, washed and dried (about 12 leaves)

12 shiso or perilla leaves (available at most Asian markets; optional)

1 cup cooked rice (preferably short grain; optional)

½ cup ssamjang, homemade (page 171) or store-bought (optional)

If you've ever wanted to capture the tantalizing flavor of Korean barbecue in your own home, look no further. My inspiration for this dish, *bulgogi*, typically calls for tougher cuts of meat, thinly sliced and marinated before being cooked through to achieve tenderness. With gently cooked sous vide steak, tenderness is guaranteed, so I've converted the original's delicious tangy, sweet, and savory marinade into a glaze that can be brushed on a finished steak to achieve the same effect. Ssamjang is a salty, rich condiment that's essential for traditional Korean barbecue. Because my recipe makes a generous amount of glaze, I've made the ssamjang optional, but it is readily available in Asian markets and online (as are perilla and shiso leaves)—and I've also included a simple recipe for making your own.

Remove the cooked steak from the bag, reserving any liquid in the bag. Thoroughly pat the steak dry with paper towels. Set aside.

MAKE THE MARINADE: In a small pot, combine the pear nectar, soy sauce, honey, garlic, ginger, green onions (white and light green parts only), sesame oil, and black pepper, along with the cooking liquid from the beef. Bring to a boil over medium heat and cook until the mixture is reduced by half and coats the back of a spoon, 3 to 5 minutes. Remove from the heat.

Preheat a grill pan or skillet over medium-high heat. Brush the steak generously on both sides with the marinade. Lightly oil the grill. Working in batches if necessary, sear the steaks until caramelized and crisp on the edges, flipping every 1 minute, for a total of 3 to 4 minutes. Transfer the cooked steaks to a cutting board and brush or drizzle on any remaining glaze. Let the steaks rest for about 5 minutes before slicing them crosswise, against the grain. Transfer meat to a platter and sprinkle with the sesame seeds and reserved green onions.

Arrange the lettuce and shiso leaves on a platter, along with bowls of the cooked rice and ssamjang. Serve family style, allowing people to assemble the wraps themselves, or do it for them: smear a small amount of ssamjang on each lettuce leaf, followed by a shiso leaf, a small amount of rice, and a few slices of steak. In either case, eaters will wrap the lettuce leaf around the fillings, creating a bundle—in Korea, it's customary to eat the wrap in one big bite, but I won't think less of you if you take two or three.

SOUS VIDE COOKING TIME
18 hours (or up to 30 hours)

———

3 pounds boneless chuck steak
(flatiron) or top sirloin (coulotte),
no more than 1½ inches thick, left
whole or cut into 1-½-inch cubes
(see individual spin-off recipes
for guidance)

Salt

———

BRAISED BEEF

Few meals say "comfort food" as emphatically as a pot roast or beef stew slowly simmered for hours until fork-tender. Based on the fact that this kind of hearty, rib-sticking fare is found in many cuisines around the world, the appeal must be pretty universal. Yet what doesn't always appeal is the need to tend a pot for hours. Sous vide to the rescue! Its slow-and-low process allows the meat's collagen to turn into gelatin, tenderizing beef—particularly the tough cuts typically called for in braises—without the risk of drying it out. Cooking the beef in advance also front-loads the preparation time and streamlines cooking more elaborate dishes like a traditional Sunday ragù from the better part of a day down to an hour or less.

A variety of different cuts will work for the spin-off dishes in this section (see Shopping Tip, facing page), and happily, the ones that work best are both flavorful and affordable. However, be sure to consult each recipe all the way through before you go the store. Unique to this section, some recipes, such as the ragù (page 93) and the Massaman curry (page 96), call for beef that is cubed before cooking sous vide, while the pot roast meat is left whole. The master recipe's initial cooking time also varies slightly, depending on what stage it becomes incorporated into the finished dishes. Follow these caveats and I promise you'll be cooking like a *nonna* in no time—with plenty of time to actual spend with your *famiglia*.

Preheat the water bath to 65°C (149°F).

Season the beef with salt and place in a 1-gallon freezer-safe ziplock bag or a vacuum seal bag. Arrange the meat in a single layer with as little overlap as possible to ensure even cooking. Seal the bag using either the water displacement method (page 12) or a vacuum sealer.

When the water reaches the target temperature, lower the bagged beef in the water bath (making sure the bag is fully submerged) and cook for 18 hours (or up to 30 hours). I recommend covering the bath with plastic wrap or aluminum foil to minimize evaporation (see page 16 for explanation) and ensure that the bag remains fully submerged the entire time.

Remove the bag from the water bath, transfer it to an ice water bath (page 18), and chill until completely cold, about 30 minutes. Once cooked and chilled, the beef can be refrigerated in the bag for up to 2 weeks.

Alternatively, if you plan on using the just-cooked beef in a spin-off recipe right away, let it rest in the bag for at least 10 minutes or up to 1 hour before proceeding.

BATCH COOKING

Because this master recipe (along with the Slow-Cooked Pork, page 68) requires longer—albeit hands-off—cooking time, and also because it makes excellent leftovers, I call for cooking a larger amount. If you don't eat it all at once, seal the leftovers in the bag using the water displacement method (page 12) or a vacuum sealer and store in the refrigerator for up to 1 week or the freezer for up to 1 month. To reheat, warm in a 65°C (149°F) water bath for 30 minutes, massaging the bag with your fingertips after 15 minutes to distribute the contents and ensure even reheating.

SHOPPING TIP

Be careful when selecting the cut of beef for these dishes: cuts that are too lean or that have too little connective tissue (think filet) will become dry after such a long cook, whereas certain tougher cuts (think short rib or shank) will require even more time to become tender. The cuts that hit the sweet spot include those from the chuck (shoulder), which are sometimes sold as "chuck steak" (flatiron steak is also a specific chuck cut), or top sirloin (culotte, aka sirloin cap, is a specific top sirloin cut). If the recipe calls for cubed beef, tri-tip is another great choice.

ADDITIONAL SPIN-OFF IDEAS

This braised beef is terrific for any beef stew recipe—just quickly brown in it a pan and add it to the pot toward the end when it's simmering, rather than at the beginning. You could also chop the meat and use it in a hash, or shred it for *ropa vieja*, the beloved beef dish from Cuba.

BEEF BOURGUIGNON POT ROAST

SERVES 6

🕐 30 MINUTES

1 MASTER RECIPE Braised Beef (page 86; made with whole top sirloin or chuck), just cooked or straight from the fridge

4 tablespoons all-purpose flour

2 tablespoons unsalted butter

4 ounces bacon, cut horizontally into ¼-inch strips

1 large shallot, minced

3 cloves garlic, minced

8 ounces cremini or button mushrooms, stems trimmed, quartered

3 tablespoons tomato paste

1½ cups light-bodied dry red wine, such as Beaujolais

1½ cup beef stock, homemade (page 176) or store-bought broth

½ cup drained cocktail onions or thawed frozen pearl onions

1 teaspoon fresh thyme leaves

Salt and freshly ground black pepper

2 tablespoons chopped fresh parsley, for garnish

Whenever I think of boeuf à la Bourguignon, I can't help but hear Julia Child's lilting, reedy voice proclaiming it "one of the most delicious beef dishes concocted by man." Whether or not the voices in your head match mine, Julia was right—this luscious stew, rising from Burgundy's peasant fare to the pantheon of French haute cuisine, is undeniably irresistible. Though commonly prepared as a stew, with small chunks of meat, I like using a single large piece and serving it as pot roast Bourguignon for a more dramatic presentation. Another untraditional twist is to use cocktail onions, which add a sweet tanginess to the dish, but frozen pearl onions certainly work as well. Serve with mashed potatoes, plain white rice, or buttered egg noodles so that none of the delicious beef juice goes to waste.

Remove the cooked braised beef from the bag, reserving any liquid in the bag. Thoroughly pat the beef dry with paper towels. Dust the beef with 1 tablespoon of the flour, patting it to form an even layer and shaking off excess. Set aside on a plate or tray.

Line a plate with paper towels and set aside.

Melt 1 tablespoon of the butter over medium heat in skillet or sauté pan large enough to fit the pot roast, until sizzling but not browned. Add the bacon and cook, stirring occasionally, until the bacon has rendered fat and is beginning to turn brown (but not crispy), 2 to 3 minutes. Remove the bacon from the pan with a slotted spoon, leaving behind the rendered fat, and transfer to the paper towel–lined plate. Set aside.

Increase the heat to high. Add the floured beef and sear, turning once, until deep golden brown, about 2 to 3 minutes per side. Lower the heat to medium and transfer the beef to a plate. Set aside.

Add the remaining 1 tablespoon of butter, the shallot, and garlic to the pan and cook, stirring constantly, for 30 seconds. Stir in the mushrooms and let them cook, stirring occasionally, until their liquid has been released and evaporated, 2 to 3 minutes. Stir in the tomato paste and cook 2 to 3 minutes more, stirring frequently until it takes on a darker shade, then add the remaining 2 tablespoons of flour and cook 1 minute longer.

Pour in the red wine while stirring, scraping any brown bits at the bottom of the pan to deglaze. Bring the mixture to a boil and cook for 1 minute, then stir in the reserved beef cooking juices, the beef stock, cocktail onions, and thyme. Allow the mixture to return to a boil and then lower the heat to a simmer. Stir in the reserved bacon, then season to taste with salt and pepper.

CONTINUED >

BEEF BOURGUIGNON POT ROAST
CONTINUED

Return the seared beef to the pan, spooning over the sauce to coat if necessary. Simmer for 3 minutes, flip the beef, and simmer for another 3 minutes. At this point you should be able to easily pierce the beef with a fork or knife (meaning it is heated through), and the sauce should be thick enough to coat the back of a spoon. If the sauce hasn't fully thickened, simmer 1 to 5 minutes longer.

Once the stew is ready, use tongs to transfer the beef to a cutting board (letting any excess sauce drip back into the pan), and slice it into ¼-inch-thick slices against the grain. Transfer the beef to a large serving platter, spooning the sauce over and around the slices, and garnish with the parsley.

BEEF RAGÙ
WITH PAPPARDELLE

Beef ragù need not be confined to an all-day undertaking requiring hours of watching and stirring. Cooking the beef sous vide ahead of time means you can have all the meaty richness of the traditional version in under an hour of active cooking (just don't tell *nonna*). Pappardelle (wide egg noodles) make an ideal vehicle for this rich, hearty ragù, and dried versions are convenient and delicious. If you want to use other shapes, the nooks and crannies of fusilli or orecchiette are also a great match—though you'll need to use 2 pounds for an equivalent number of servings, as these semolina-based pastas absorb less water than pappardelle.

This recipe makes enough to serve a crowd, but if you're cooking for a smaller number of people, I encourage you to halve the quantity of pasta and save the excess ragù for another time—it's perfectly delicious reheated (see Batch Cooking on page 87). Once chilled, the ragù can be stored in the refrigerator for up to 1 week or the freezer for up to 1 month, and then reheated at 65°C (149°F).

Remove the cooked braised beef from the bag, reserving any liquid in the bag. Thoroughly pat the beef dry with paper towels.

Heat 3 tablespoons of the olive oil in a large Dutch oven or wide-bottomed pot over medium-high heat, until the oil is shimmering and giving off wisps of smoke. Working in batches if necessary, add the cooked beef pieces so that they fit in one layer without overcrowding and sear, turning once until deep golden brown, 2 to 3 minutes per side. Once browned, transfer the beef to a plate. Set aside.

Add the carrot, onion, and celery to the pan, season with a pinch of salt, and stir, scraping with a wooden spoon to release any brown bits from the bottom of the pan. Cook, stirring occasionally, until the vegetables are softened and golden brown, 5 to 6 minutes. Use a wooden spoon to push the vegetables to one side of the pot, leaving the bottom partially exposed. Add the remaining 1 tablespoon of olive oil, followed by the garlic. Continue to cook, stirring occasionally, until the garlic begins to turn light golden brown, 1 to 2 minutes, then add the anchovy, red pepper flakes, and rosemary, and cook about 30 seconds more, until the mixture is aromatic and the anchovy has begun to dissolve.

Stir the vegetables back to the center of the pan to combine with the garlic mixture, then add the red wine to deglaze. Bring the wine to a boil and cook

SERVES 6 TO 8
🕐 50 MINUTES

1 MASTER RECIPE Braised Beef (page 86; made with chuck steak, top sirloin, or tri-tip, cubed and cooked for at least 24 hours), just cooked or straight from the fridge

4 tablespoons extra-virgin olive oil

1 carrot, peeled and cut into ¼-inch dice

1 onion, cut into ¼-inch dice

1 celery stalk, cut into ¼-inch dice

Salt and freshly ground black pepper

3 cloves garlic, thinly sliced

3 anchovy fillets, or 1½ teaspoons anchovy paste (optional)

Pinch of red pepper flakes, or as needed

2 teaspoons chopped rosemary

1 cup dry red wine

1 (28-ounce) can crushed tomatoes (preferably San Marzano)

500 grams (17.6 ounces) dried egg pappardelle

¼ cup grated Pecorino or Parmesan cheese, for garnish

2 tablespoons chopped fresh parsley, for garnish

CONTINUED >

BEEF RAGÙ WITH PAPPARDELLE

for 1 minute, then stir in the crushed tomatoes, reserved cooking juices, and the browned beef.

Bring the mixture to a boil, then reduce heat to a simmer and cook, uncovered, stirring occasionally, for 35 to 40 minutes, until the beef is falling apart into the sauce. (While the sauce simmers, use the back of a wooden spoon to press the beef pieces against the side of the pot to help break them up.)

Remove the sauce from the heat and season to taste with additional salt and pepper.

While the ragù is simmering, bring a large pot of water to a boil. Season the water generously with salt. Once you're ready to serve, cook the pasta to al dente according to the package instructions, then drain it thoroughly in a colander.

In a large bowl, toss the pasta with the ragù, reserving 1 to 2 cups of the ragù. Spoon the reserved ragù over the top of the pasta, then garnish with the grated Pecorino and parsley.

Because you want the beef in this recipe to be completely fall-apart tender, rather than just fork-tender, it works best when the beef is cooked longer than for the other spin-off recipes—at least 24 hours, rather than the minimum 18 hours.

MASSAMAN CURRY

SERVES 6 GENEROUSLY
🕐 15 MINUTES

1 tablespoon coconut, peanut, or vegetable oil

1 (4-ounce) can Maesri massaman curry paste

1 yellow onion, cut into ½-inch dice

2 (13.5-ounce) cans coconut milk (do not shake before opening)

1 pound small, waxy potatoes (such as baby red bliss, fingerlings, or German butterballs), halved

1 or 2 star anise pods

2 bay leaves

1 (2-inch) cinnamon stick

1 MASTER RECIPE Braised Beef (page 86; made with chuck steak, top sirloin cut, or tri-tip, cubed), just cooked or straight from the fridge

¼ cup roasted unsalted peanuts, plus more for garnish

2 or 3 tablespoons fish sauce

1 or 2 tablespoons lime juice

Massaman curry is a delicious example of culinary fusion: its name refers to Muslim immigrants to Thailand who brought their food traditions with them. At the heart of this dish is massaman curry paste, which boasts the dry spices found in Middle Eastern and Indian cuisines (such as cumin, cinnamon, and cardamom), as well as the fresh spices typical of Thai cuisine (such as galangal and lemongrass). All the wonderful complexity of this dish is achieved with ease using store-bought curry paste. I call for a specific brand, Maesri, which is readily available at Asian markets and in well-stocked Asian food aisles in grocery stores. I don't recommend using a different brand, since others will require adjustments and additional ingredients such as sugar or tamarind to achieve success with this dish. Steamed jasmine rice makes the perfect side.

Heat the oil in a large Dutch oven or stockpot over medium-high heat, until shimmering. Add the curry paste and onion and cook for 1 minute, stirring constantly, until fragrant.

Skim off the thick layer at the top of each can of coconut milk (the "cream") and add it to the pot, reserving the thinner liquid beneath it to add later. Cook the mixture until it's bubbling and the oil is beginning to separate, about 2 minutes more.

Add the reserved coconut milk and bring the mixture to a boil. Reduce the heat to a simmer, then add the potatoes, star anise, bay leaves, and cinnamon stick. If necessary, add water so that the potatoes are just covered. Simmer for about 15 minutes, until the potatoes are tender.

Add the cooked beef to the pot, along with any of its reserved cooking juices, and return the mixture to a simmer. Stir in the ¼ cup of peanuts and cook for 2 minutes, to ensure the beef is heated through, then remove from the heat. Season to taste with the fish sauce and lime juice. Remove the whole spices, if desired.

Ladle into bowls and garnish with the additional peanuts, if desired.

DELUXE STUFFED CHEESEBURGER

SERVES 4

SOUS VIDE COOKING TIME
🕐 1 hour (or up to 5 hours)

ACTIVE COOKING TIME
🕐 20 minutes

BURGER PATTIES

3 ounces sharp Cheddar or Gruyère, or a mix, finely grated (about ¾ cup)

2 tablespoons unsalted butter, at room temperature

2 pounds lean ground beef (85 or 90% lean)

Salt

"SECRET" SAUCE

2 tablespoons mayonnaise, homemade (page 172) or store-bought

1 tablespoon ketchup

1 tablespoon Dijon mustard

1 teaspoon Worcestershire sauce

Freshly ground black pepper, plus more for patties

4 hamburger buns, split (toasted if desired)

12 dill pickle coins

8 leaves Bibb or iceberg lettuce

4 thin slices ripe beefsteak-type tomato, from 1 tomato

I couldn't resist sharing the recipe for this next-level cheeseburger: cooked medium rare from edge to edge, it reveals a gloriously oozy center once you take a bite. The inspiration for this cheese-filled wonder is the Jucy Lucy, the iconic burger of Minneapolis—my coauthor and recipe writer Scott's hometown. According to him, some controversy surrounds the proper [mis] spelling; two separate south Minneapolis bars claim to have invented the dish, and each insists on a particular spelling (Jucy vs. Juicy). I'll leave the verdict on that to the court of public opinion. What's not up for debate is that this is a seriously indulgent three-napkin affair.

Preheat the water bath to 57°C (134.6°F).

MAKE THE BURGER PATTIES: In a small bowl, combine the cheese and 1 tablespoon of the butter and mix with a wooden spoon until well blended and no flecks of butter are visible.

Divide the ground beef into 8 equal portions, each about 4 ounces. Using your hands, roll each portion into a ball, then shape into a flattened disk about 5 to 6 inches across and ½ inch thick. Using your thumb, press a shallow indentation about the size of a silver dollar (1½-inch diameter) into the center of 4 of the patties, and spoon a quarter of the cheese mix (about 2 tablespoons) into each. Place the remaining 4 patties on top and press both halves together firmly, pinching the edges and handling as needed so that the edges are sealed and the resulting patties are approximately ¾ inch thick and 5 to 6 inches in diameter. Season your shaped burger patties with salt (see page 25).

Place the shaped cheeseburger patties in a 1-gallon freezer-safe ziplock bag or a vacuum seal bag. Arrange the patties in a single layer with as little overlap as possible to ensure even cooking. Seal the bag using either the water displacement method (page 12) or a vacuum sealer.

When the water reaches the target temperature, lower the bagged cheeseburgers in the water bath (making sure the bag is fully submerged) and cook for 1 hour (or up to 5 hours).

Remove the bag from the water bath, transfer it to an ice water bath (page 18), and chill until completely cold, about 20 minutes. Once cooked and chilled, the burgers can be refrigerated in the bag for up to 2 weeks.

If you plan on preparing the cheeseburgers right away, let them rest in the sealed bag at room temperature for at least 10 minutes, or up to an hour, before proceeding. Allowing the surface of the cheeseburgers to

CONTINUED >

DELUXE STUFFED CHEESEBURGER
CONTINUED

cool a bit before grilling them ensures that the meat won't overcook or develop that dreaded grey band in the final step.

Alternatively, if you plan to prepare the cheeseburger in advance to serve later (see box for tips), transfer the bag to an ice water bath (page 18) and chill until completely cold, about 20 minutes, before refrigerating. The chilled burgers can be refrigerated in the bag for up to 2 weeks.

MAKE THE "SECRET" SAUCE: While the cheeseburgers are resting, whisk together the mayonnaise, ketchup, mustard, and Worcestershire sauce in a small bowl and season to taste with freshly ground black pepper. Set aside. This sauce will keep for several weeks in a tightly sealed container in the fridge, so feel free to double or triple the quantity to have it on hand.

Remove the cheeseburger patties from the bag, discarding any liquid in the bag. Thoroughly pat the cheeseburgers dry with paper towels. Season the patties with additional freshly ground pepper, if desired.

Preheat a cast-iron skillet or griddle over medium-high heat. Add the remaining 1 tablespoon of butter to the pan (it should sizzle and begin to brown immediately), then immediately place the cheeseburger patties in the pan and cook just until a dark brown crust forms, 2 to 3 minutes per side. Once the burgers are heated through, the middle will dome slightly, indicating that the cheese inside is properly melted and the cheeseburgers are done.

If you're reheating the patties straight from the refrigerator, increase the cooking time by 2 to 3 minutes, for a total of 6 to 9 minutes, flipping as needed to avoid overbrowning.

Transfer the seared cheeseburger patties onto a plate or tray. (If toasting your burger buns, you can do so now, placing both halves, cut side down, into the pan with any remaining fat, until browned and crisped, 30 seconds to 1 minute.) Assemble the burgers by spreading 1 generous tablespoon of the "secret" sauce between the bottom halves of the buns, followed by 3 pickle coins, 2 leaves of lettuce, 1 tomato slice, 1 burger, and lastly the top bun.

TAILGATING TIPS

Because these cheeseburgers can easily be cooked in advance without sacrificing their magic, they work wonderfully for a really impressive cookout burger. If you're finishing them on an outdoor grill, make sure the grill is well oiled, omit the second tablespoon of butter, and sear for the same amount of time to reheat from cold.

HOLD THE CHEESE

This approach is also excellent for standard, unfilled patties—cooking them sous vide ensures the juiciest, most tender medium-rare burgers without fear of under- or overcooking them. Simply form the meat into 4 (8-ounce) patties and proceed with the seasoning and cooking instructions.

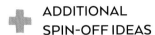

ADDITIONAL SPIN-OFF IDEAS

The possible variations for this burger are limitless. Play around with the different kinds of fillings, proteins, and toppings. Meltier cheese options such as Swiss or Fontina (or even, gasp, American), crumbly options like feta or Parmesan, or even blue cheeses will work deliciously well. For a Greek spin, try ground lamb patties stuffed with feta served with a "secret" sauce jazzed up with a pinch of ground cumin and minced garlic. If you're avoiding red meat, substitute ground dark-meat turkey and cook for the same amount of time, but increase the cooking temperature to 65°C (149°F).

SHRIMP AND FISH

1 pound large shrimp, peeled and deveined (approximately 16 to 20), with the tails left on if desired

Salt

SHRIMP

Shrimp is America's favorite seafood, hitting a sweet spot between affordability and outright luxury, making it an everyday option that still feels indulgent. After paying a pretty penny for your precious catch, however, the last thing you want to do is overcook it. Like other types of seafood, shrimp is highly sensitive to heat and goes from raw to rubbery in a matter of minutes. With an immersion circulator at your disposal, you can control the temperature of the water bath so you don't need advanced culinary training to prepare shrimp flawlessly. After discovering how easy it is to make juicy firm-yet-tender shrimp using the gentle, precise heat of sous vide, you'll never go back to settling for a lackluster seafood cocktail or sad take-out lo mein again.

Best of all, shrimp cooked in this method take only about 15 minutes, so you can easily prep the rest of the ingredients in the spin-off recipes, like my not-exactly-traditional gumbo or a garlicky scampi-style linguine, while they're bobbing away merrily in the bath. Even when prepared ahead of time, you never have to worry about the shrimp turning tough in the final dish—all they need a minute or two of heat to gently warm through before serving.

Preheat the water bath to 60°C (140°F).

Season the shrimp lightly with salt and place in a 1-gallon freezer-safe ziplock bag or a vacuum seal bag. Arrange the shrimp in a single layer with as little overlap as possible to ensure even cooking. Seal the bag using either the water displacement method (page 12) or a vacuum sealer.

When the water reaches the target temperature, lower the bagged shrimp in the water bath (making sure the bag is fully submerged) and cook for 15 minutes (or up to 25 minutes).

Remove the bag from the water bath, transfer it to an ice water bath (see page 18), and chill until completely cold, about 10 minutes. Once cooked and chilled, the shrimp can be refrigerated in the bag for up to 1 week.

Alternatively, if you plan on using the just-cooked shrimp in a spin-off recipe right away, let them rest in the bag at room temperature for at least 10 minutes or up to 1 hour before proceeding.

BATCH COOKING

If doubling this recipe, you can safely fit all the shrimp in a 1-gallon bag. Just be sure to arrange them in a single layer with as little overlap as possible to ensure even cooking. If you're increasing the quantity beyond that, use two bags.

SHOPPING TIP

The recipes in this chapter call for large shrimp, which are sometimes marketed at the fish counter as $16/20$—meaning there are between 16 and 20 shrimp per pound. Slightly smaller shrimp, classified as $21/25$, will also work for these recipes without adjustment. If you can get your hands only on shrimp that are significantly larger or smaller, you'll still get excellent results, but you will need to adjust the cooking time. For instance, tiny bay shrimp, which are 1 inch long at the most, will take as few as 5 minutes, whereas the largest sizes, often marketed as colossal or prawn, come as few as 4 to 6 per pound and will take closer to 25 minutes.

ADDITIONAL SPIN-OFF IDEAS

These shrimp would be fantastic in a chilled salad, dressed with dill, lemon, and mayonnaise; added at the last minute to a Chinese stir-fry; or slipped into a bowl of piping-hot Thai hot and sour soup just before serving to heat them through.

SHRIMP
WITH CLASSIC COCKTAIL SAUCE

Shrimp cocktail is a dish familiar to almost everyone, but it very rarely dazzles. No amount of cocktail sauce, no matter how punchy or delicious it is, will manage to completely cover up the flaws of unremarkable or overcooked shrimp. The succulent tender texture and pure flavor of shrimp cooked sous vide makes for unbeatable cocktail shrimp, and my zippy version of a classic cocktail sauce serves to enhance, rather than distract from that. If you haven't already cooled the shrimp in the ice bath, refrigerate for at least 1 hour before serving.

Chill four to six cocktail glasses in the refrigerator for at least at least 30 minutes.

MAKE THE COCKTAIL SAUCE: Combine the ketchup, horseradish, mustard, lemon juice, Worcestershire sauce, Tabasco, and black pepper in a medium bowl and whisk to mix well. Divide the sauce evenly among the chilled martini glasses.

Remove the chilled shrimp from the bag using a slotted spoon, transfer to a plate, and thoroughly pat dry with paper towels. Discard the liquid in the bag.

Divide the shrimp among the cocktail sauce–filled martini glasses, arranging each shrimp so that it hangs over the lip of the glass, tail facing outward. Sprinkle with the parsley and serve immediately.

**SERVES 4 TO 6
AS AN APPETIZER
🕑 5 MINUTES**

COCKTAIL SAUCE
MAKES ¾ CUP

½ cup ketchup

1 tablespoon horseradish, freshly grated or prepared

1 tablespoon Dijon mustard

1 tablespoon lemon juice

1 teaspoon Worcestershire sauce

1 or 2 teaspoons Tabasco or other hot sauce

½ teaspoon freshly ground black pepper

1 MASTER RECIPE Shrimp (page 104), just cooked and chilled or straight from the fridge chilled

1 tablespoon chopped fresh Italian parsley, for garnish

GARLICKY SHRIMP LINGUINE

I based this recipe on the paradoxically named shrimp scampi—paradoxical because *scampi* is actually the Italian word for *langoustine*, or Norway lobster, a different type of crustacean altogether. In practice, the name refers to an Italian-American dish of shrimp cooked in a garlicky sauce featuring white wine and butter and typically served over pasta. This combination is a winner no matter what you want to call it—it's easy enough for a weekday but decadent enough for entertaining.

While combining cheese and seafood is generally frowned upon in Italian cuisine, I think the mildness of ricotta salata (literally "salted ricotta") complements the shrimp nicely. The pickled hot cherry peppers—available at most Italian markets—are also an unconventional touch, but worth seeking out, as they add a nice pop of heat and acidity. Leftover pickled peppers are a great add-on for pizzas, salads, or a salumi platter.

Bring a large pot of water to a boil and season generously with salt. Cook the linguine to al dente according to the package instructions.

While the pasta is cooking, heat the olive oil and 2 tablespoons of the butter in a sauté pan over medium heat until the butter is melted and just begins to bubble. Add the garlic and pickled cherry peppers and cook, stirring constantly, until fragrant and sizzling, making sure the garlic doesn't brown, 1 to 2 minutes. Add the wine to the pan and simmer until reduced in half, about 2 minutes.

Remove the chilled shrimp from the bag and transfer them, along with any liquid in the bag, to the pan. Return the mixture to a simmer and cook for 1 minute or just until the shrimp are fully heated, then immediately remove from the heat. Stir in the remaining 1 tablespoon of butter along with the lemon zest, lemon juice, and black pepper. Season with additional salt to taste.

Drain the cooked pasta in a colander and transfer it to a large bowl. Add the shrimp and the ¼ cup of chopped parsley and toss lightly to coat the pasta. Sprinkle with the ricotta salata and additional parsley and serve immediately.

SERVES 4
⏱ 20 MINUTES

Salt

1 pound linguine

3 tablespoons extra-virgin olive oil

3 tablespoons unsalted butter

5 cloves garlic, thinly sliced

1 to 2 tablespoons minced pickled hot cherry peppers or a generous pinch of red pepper flakes

½ cup dry white wine

1 MASTER RECIPE Shrimp (page 104), just cooked or straight from the fridge

Zest of ½ lemon, finely grated

2 tablespoons freshly squeezed lemon juice

Freshly ground black pepper

¼ cup chopped fresh Italian parsley, plus additional for garnish

¼ cup coarsely grated ricotta salata or queso fresco, for garnish (optional)

SHRIMP GUMBO

SERVES 4 TO 6

🕐 30 MINUTES

2 tablespoons canola or other neutral vegetable oil

8 ounces andouille or other smoked sausage, cut into ¼-inch slices

2 tablespoons unsalted butter

1 green bell pepper, cut into ½-inch dice

1 medium white or yellow onion, cut into ½-inch dice

2 celery stalks, cut into ½-inch dice

3 cloves garlic, minced

3 tablespoons all-purpose flour

1 (6-ounce) can tomato paste

2 quarts chicken broth, homemade (page 176) or low-sodium store-bought broth

15 small okra pods, stemmed and cut into ¼-inch slices (about 1 cup; optional)

1 tablespoon Creole seasoning

⅓ cup coarsely chopped fresh Italian parsley, plus additional for garnish

2 teaspoons cider vinegar

Salt and freshly ground black pepper

Tabasco or other hot sauce (optional)

1 MASTER RECIPE Shrimp (page 104), just cooked or straight from the fridge

Gumbo is the grande dame of Cajun Creole cuisine, boasting a mélange of culinary influences, including native Choctaw, French, Spanish, and West African. Traditional gumbo is an involved affair, and while my version certainly isn't traditional, it satisfies any cravings for a taste of Louisiana—and it comes together quickly. If you're not a fan of okra, feel free to leave it out. Steamed rice and cornbread are the perfect complements.

In a large Dutch oven or casserole, heat the oil over high heat until it shimmers and gives off wisps of smoke. Add the andouille sausage and cook, stirring occasionally, until the edges are browned, 1 to 2 minutes. Stir in the butter, which should immediately sizzle, and cook until it browns and begins to smelly nutty, about 1 minute.

Reduce the heat to medium and add the bell pepper, onion, and celery and cook until the vegetables begin to soften and brown, 4 to 5 minutes. Stir in the garlic and cook 1 minute more. Stir in the flour followed by the tomato paste and cook for 2 to 3 minutes more, stirring constantly to avoid scorching, until the tomato paste has turned a shade darker.

Pour the chicken broth into the pot in a steady stream, stirring constantly, to prevent clumping. Bring the mixture to a boil, then lower the heat to a simmer. Stir in the okra, along with the Creole seasoning, the ⅓ cup parsley, and the vinegar. Season to taste with salt and pepper, along with a dash or two of Tabasco, then continue to simmer until all of the vegetables have softened, about 10 minutes more. Remove the pan from the heat.

Remove the chilled shrimp from the bag and transfer them, along with any liquid in the bag, into the pot and stir. The heat of the stew is enough to warm up the shrimp; if they are coming directly from the refrigerator, allow a few extra minutes before serving.

Garnish with the additional chopped parsley and serve.

SOUS VIDE COOKING TIME
20 minutes (or up to 30 minutes;
an additional 20 to 30 minutes
if brining)

ALL-PURPOSE SEAFOOD
BRINE (OPTIONAL)
MAKES 2 CUPS

2 cups water

¼ cup salt

1 tablespoon sugar (optional)

1½ pounds salmon fillet
(1 to 1½ inches thick at the widest
point), pin bones removed, skin
removed (optional), cut into
4 equal pieces

Salt (if not using brine)

1 teaspoon canola or
other neutral vegetable oil

SALMON

You'll never again need to fear overcooking your fish; because the fish's internal temperature never rises above the setting of the water bath, it's impossible to dry out your catch. In this chapter, I call for cooking salmon at 52.5°C (126.5°F), which to me delivers the best possible texture. Feel free to increase or decrease the temperature to suit your own taste. At 43.3°C (109.9°F), fish is heated through but has a sushi-like texture, while at 60°C (140°F) results in a flakier and firmer texture while still retaining moisture.

Because sous vide fish is more delicate than conventionally cooked fish, it's harder to handle, which is why I call for portioning your food before you cook it. Salmon cooked this way is also easier to handle when it's cold. Preparing the master recipe ahead of time not only offers you last-minute convenience, but also makes the final preparation of the spin-off recipes— be it searing, stir-frying, or flaking into a salad—that much easier.

Preheat the water bath to 52.5°C (126.5°F).

IF BRINING: In a small bowl, mix together the water, salt, and sugar, stirring until the salt and sugar are completely dissolved. Place the salmon fillets in a 1-gallon freezer-safe ziplock bag, add the brine, seal the bag (no need to vacuum), and let rest in the fridge for 20 to 30 minutes. Leaving the fish in the bag, pour out the brining liquid, add the oil to the bag, and rub all over the surface of the fish to coat.

IF NOT BRINING: Season the salmon with salt and rub it with enough oil to coat. Place the salmon in a 1-gallon freezer-safe ziplock bag and arrange in a single layer with as little overlap as possible to ensure even cooking.

Seal the bag using either the water displacement method (page 12) or a vacuum sealer.

When the water reaches the target temperature, lower the bagged salmon in the water bath (making sure the bag is fully submerged) and cook for 20 minutes (or up to 30 minutes). When the fish is done it will be an opaque pink color and very delicate, so handle it with care or it will fall apart.

Remove the bag from the water bath, transfer to an ice water bath (page 18), and chill until completely cold, about 20 minutes. Once cooked and chilled, the salmon can be refrigerated in the bag for up to 5 days.

Alternatively, if you plan on using the just-cooked salmon in a spin-off recipe right away, let it rest in the bag for at least 10 minutes or up to 1 hour before proceeding.

COOKING TIP

Another trick to bring your salmon to the next level is to brine it before cooking. This not only seasons the fish, but it also firms up the texture and prevents the flesh from releasing albumens, that unappetizing-looking white ooze that often appears on the exterior of cooked fish. The brining step, if you choose to use it, is pretty quick and effortless, and once you've tried it with salmon, you may want to put it to use when cooking other types of fish (see Flaky White Fish, page 120). If you decide to skip the brining step, simply season the fish lightly with salt in the bag before cooking it into the water bath.

SHOPPING TIP

This recipe works equally well for any variety of salmon, including coho, king/Chinook, and sockeye, as well as Arctic char.

ADDITIONAL SPIN-OFF IDEAS

Flake pieces of chilled salmon over a plate of greens, potatoes, and Nicoise olives for a salmon Nicoise, or sear on a grill and top with a compound herbed butter.

SEARED FIVE-SPICE SALMON
WITH STIR-FRIED SNOW PEAS

SERVES 4

🕐 **10 MINUTES**

1 MASTER RECIPE Salmon
(page 112; preferably skin-on),
brined or unbrined, just cooked
or straight from the fridge

¾ teaspoon Chinese
five-spice powder

1 tablespoon canola oil

1 teaspoon toasted sesame oil

1 tablespoon peeled, minced
fresh ginger, from about
1 (1-inch) piece

3 cloves garlic, minced

3 green onions, thinly sliced,
2 tablespoons dark green parts
reserved for garnish

2 cups snow peas or sugar snap
peas, stemmed

¼ cup Shaoxing rice wine or
dry sherry

2 tablespoons soy sauce

1 tablespoon rice vinegar

2 teaspoons sugar

This crispy salmon stir-fry is one of my favorite ways to enjoy a nearly perfect piece of salmon. Be sure to look for fillets that still have the skin on—not only are they packed with healthy omega-3 fatty acids, but once seared, the crackly crust provides a fantastic contrast to the salmon's tender flesh. This classic Chinese dish gets its intoxicating flavors from a quick pan sauce made from five-spice powder, soy sauce, and Shaoxing wine, a traditional Chinese wine fermented from glutinous rice that originates from the region of Shaoxing in eastern China. Also sold as Shaoshing, it's a popular ingredient in Chinese and Taiwanese cooking that's readily available at Asian markets and online; if you can't find it, dry sherry will work just fine. Serve with a side of warm rice.

Gently remove the cooked salmon pieces from the bag, discarding any liquid in the bag, and transfer it to a platter or tray—the fish will be very delicate, so handle it with care or it will fall apart. Thoroughly pat the salmon dry with a paper towel. If the salmon was cooked with the skin on and you would like to serve it without the skin, you can remove it now: simply start at one end and lift it off in one piece. Sprinkle the salmon on both sides with the Chinese five-spice powder.

In a large nonstick sauté pan, heat the oil over medium-high heat until shimmering. Carefully place the salmon pieces into the pan. If using skin-on salmon, lay the skin side down to get it crispy.

If using just-cooked salmon, carefully place the pieces into the pan (skin side down, if using) and cook for 1 to 2 minutes, until golden brown and crisp. Flip to give the second side a touch of heat, then remove from the pan.

If using previously chilled salmon, cook it for 2 to 3 minutes on the first side to ensure that the fish is golden brown, crisp, and thoroughly warmed through, and then flip and cook for 1 minute more. Remove from the heat and immediately transfer the salmon to plates or shallow bowls and cover (or set aside in a low oven) to keep warm. Pour off all but 1 tablespoon of fat from the pan.

Return the pan to the heat and add the sesame oil, ginger, garlic, and green onions (white and light green parts only) and cook, stirring constantly with a wooden spoon, until they become fragrant, about 30 seconds. Add the snow peas and stir-fry for 1 to 2 minutes more, just until they turn bright green. Add the Shaoxing wine, soy sauce, rice vinegar, and sugar to the pan and bring to a boil. At this point the peas should be crispy but not raw. Remove the pan from the heat.

Spoon the peas and sauce around each piece of warm salmon and sprinkle with the reserved green onions.

SALMON SALAD
WITH CREAMY DILL DRESSING

Scandinavia's love of salmon is second to none, so I followed their lead for this cold seafood dish, which highlights salmon's natural affinity for the anise-y flavors of dill and fennel. I love piling the fish on top of crisp Swedish *knäckebröd* (literally "crisp bread"), which is widely available, as are Norwegian and Danish versions. You can also serve it on sliced bread such as caraway rye, but any dense, fine-grained loaf will work. Once the salmon is cooked, the dish comes together extremely quickly, but if you haven't already cooled the salmon in the ice bath, you'll need to refrigerate it at least 1 hour before serving.

MAKE THE DRESSING: In a bowl large enough to hold the salmon, whisk together the mustard, lemon juice, shallot, and salt and set aside for 5 minutes (this will mellow the taste of the shallot). Add the fennel seed, yogurt, olive oil, and ¼ cup of the dill and whisk until the olive oil is fully incorporated. Season with the salt and white pepper to taste.

Open the bag of cooked, chilled salmon and pour out the liquid, leaving the fish behind. Use your fingertips to gently break apart the salmon into large flakes—they'll break down further when mixed with the dressing.

Using a wooden spoon or rubber spatula, gently fold the cooked salmon into the bowl with the dressing until the pieces are just coated, taking care not to overmix—you want some larger flakes of salmon to remain.

Butter the bread and evenly spoon a generous heap of the dressed salmon salad onto each slice—you want a lot of luscious salmon in each bite. Place the fennel slices and reserved dill sprigs on top and finish with a squeeze of lemon juice and a sprinkle of flaky salt.

SERVES 4
🕐 **15 MINUTES**

CREAMY DILL DRESSING

1 tablespoon grainy mustard

1 tablespoon freshly squeezed lemon juice

1 small shallot, minced

Pinch of salt

½ teaspoon ground fennel seed (optional)

½ cup whole milk Greek yogurt or crème fraîche

3 tablespoons extra-virgin olive oil

¼ cup chopped fresh dill or fennel fronds, or a mixture of both, plus 1 tablespoon sprigs for garnish

Salt and freshly ground white pepper

1 MASTER RECIPE Salmon (page 112), brined or unbrined, chilled, skinned

4 large pieces rye crisp bread or thinly sliced rye bread

2 tablespoons salted butter, at room temperature (optional)

1 small fennel bulb or ½ large bulb, thinly sliced or mandolined (about 1 cup)

1 lemon wedge

Flaky sea salt, such as Maldon or fleur de sel

MISO-GLAZED SALMON
WITH WILTED GREENS

SERVES 4

🕐 20 MINUTES

MISO GLAZE

⅓ cup mirin

1 tablespoon rice vinegar

¼ cup white miso

2 tablespoons honey

2 teaspoons toasted sesame oil

1 MASTER RECIPE Salmon (page 112), brined or unbrined, skin off, just cooked or straight from the fridge

3 cups packed baby spinach or kale (central ribs removed), thinly sliced

Pinch of salt

1 tablespoon toasted sesame seeds, for garnish

In Japan, it's common to marinate richer fish with sweet, salty, umami-loaded miso paste, resulting in something simple but also singularly indulgent. Because richer fish will stand up better to the flavorful miso glaze, I recommend fish like salmon, but black cod or sea bass would also be a great match. Just be sure to remove the skin, because it won't get crispy beneath the glaze. The combination of healthy omega-3s from the fish and nutrient-packed greens makes this meal both healthy and satisfying as it is, but you could round it out with some brown rice for added heft.

Preheat the broiler to medium with the rack placed in the middle, about 6 inches from the heat.

MAKE THE GLAZE: In a small saucepan, add the mirin and rice vinegar and bring to a boil over medium heat. Whisk in the white miso and honey and cook until the mixture has formed a glaze thick enough to coat the back of a spoon, 1 to 2 minutes. Remove from heat and whisk in 1 teaspoon of the sesame oil.

Gently remove the cooked salmon pieces from the bag, discarding any liquid in the bag, and transfer the fish to a plate or tray—the fish will be very delicate, so handle it with care or it will fall apart. Thoroughly pat the salmon dry with paper towels.

Place the fillets flat side down into a large, ovenproof nonstick sauté pan or baking dish, and spoon or brush about 1 generous tablespoon of glaze over each piece, using the back of the spoon or brush to spread it evenly over the surface. (If a small amount of glaze pools around the pieces of fish, that's fine.)

Place the salmon under the broiler and cook until the glaze is bubbling, deep golden brown, and beginning to blacken around the edges, 3 to 6 minutes. The fish will have begun to flake apart and be fully cooked through. If you're using just-cooked salmon, it may take only 2 to 3 minutes to heat through, resulting in a lighter color. Remove the pan from the oven and transfer the glazed fillets to a large plate or tray. If any of the glaze left behind on the pan has gotten too burnt, wipe it off with a paper towel.

Add the spinach or kale, remaining 1 teaspoon of sesame oil, and a pinch of salt to the pan and toss, letting the residual heat of the pan wilt the greens. (If they don't wilt, pop the pan of greens under the broiler for another 30 seconds to 1 minute.)

Divide the wilted greens evenly between individual plates or bowls and top with a piece of glazed salmon. Using a spoon, drizzle the remaining glaze over the fish and greens and sprinkle some sesame seeds on top.

SOUS VIDE COOKING TIME
20 minutes (or up to 35 minutes;
an additional 20 to 30 minutes
if brining)

ALL-PURPOSE SEAFOOD
BRINE (OPTIONAL)
MAKES 2 CUPS

2 cups water

¼ cup salt

1 tablespoon sugar (optional)

1½ pounds boneless, skinless flaky
white fish fillet (1 to 1½ inches
thick at the widest point),
cut into 4 equal pieces

Salt (if not using brine)

1 teaspoon canola or
other neutral vegetable oil

FLAKY WHITE FISH

Whether it's flaky cod or meaty mahi mahi, cooking fish takes care. But with sous vide on your side, there's no need to have a graduate degree in *fruits de mer*—you're guaranteed great results. In this master recipe, I call for cooking flaky fish at 55°C (125.5°F). Although this is slightly higher than what I call for in the master salmon recipe (page 112), it still results in flesh that's slightly firm but still exceedingly tender and succulent. If you want to experiment with additional cuts and thicknesses, the fish will need to spend more time in the water bath (see the cooking chart on page 183 for specific instructions).

As when cooking any type of delicate fish using sous vide, I recommend you follow my best practices: brine for 20 to 30 minutes (see Cooking Tip on page 113) to firm up the flesh, remove the unseemly gooey white albumin that tends to seep out when cooking fish, and take care when handling your fish. Another tip: a nonstick pan works best when preparing the spin-off dishes in this chapter.

Preheat the water bath to 55°C (125.5°F).

IF BRINING: In a small bowl, mix together the water, salt, and sugar, stirring until the salt and sugar are completely dissolved. Place the fish fillets in a 1-gallon freezer-safe ziplock bag, add the brine, seal the bag (no need to vacuum), and let rest in the fridge for 20 to 30 minutes. Leaving the fish in the bag, pour out the brining liquid, add the oil to the bag, and rub all over the surface of the fish to coat.

IF NOT BRINING: Season the fish with salt and rub it with enough oil to coat. Place the fish in a 1-gallon freezer-safe ziplock bag and arrange the pieces in a single layer with as little overlap as possible to ensure even cooking.

Seal the bag using either the water displacement method (page 12) or a vacuum sealer.

When the water reaches the target temperature, lower the bagged fish in the water bath (making sure the bag is fully submerged) and cook for 20 minutes (or up to 35 minutes). When the fish is done it will be opaque and very delicate, so handle it with care or it will fall apart.

Remove the bag from the water bath, transfer to an ice water bath (page 18), and chill until completely cold, about 20 minutes. Once cooked and chilled, the fish can be refrigerated in the bag for up to 5 days.

Alternatively, if you plan on using the just-cooked fish in a spin-off recipe right away, let it rest in the bag at room temperature for at least 10 minutes or up to 1 hour before proceeding.

COOKING TIP

I love eating fish that still has the skin left on—the skin not only lends moisture, but it crisps up beautifully in the pan. That said, if you prefer your fish without the skin, you can still cook it sous vide with it left on. In fact it's much easier to remove the skin once it's cooked. Similarly, if you're planning on serving your flaky fish whole, it's fairly easy to remove the pin bones after it's cooked. However, if you plan on serving the fish in bite-sized pieces, as in the chowder or fish tacos, or if you plan on making a one-bag meal (see page 177), ask your fishmonger to remove the bones so you don't have to pick them out when you open the bag.

SHOPPING TIP

The time and temperature called for in this recipe will work for almost any kind of fish—sea bass, mahi mahi, snapper, cod, catfish—that's about 1 inch thick.

ADDITIONAL SPIN-OFF IDEAS

Left whole, these delicate fish fillets can be brushed with a miso glaze (page 118) and grilled, topped with a store-bought tapenade or piccata sauce (page 62), battered and deep-fried for fish and chips, or flaked over a simply dressed salad.

If using habanero peppers, exercise care when cutting them, as they can be exceptionally hot. Make sure to wear gloves or thoroughly wash your hands with soap and water after handling them, being especially mindful not to touch your face (or eyes!) immediately after working with them.

GRILLED FISH TACOS
WITH MANGO SALSA

These tacos will instantly transport you to a sunny beach in Mexico. They're big on flavor and come together quickly, leaving you more time for sipping on margaritas. Like the other spin-off dishes in this section, this recipe is ultra versatile. I think a firmer fish such as sea bass, mahi mahi, or snapper is the best fit here, but any flaky fish will work. My favorite mango varieties are Ataulfo (aka honey or Champagne) and Alphonso, for their sweetness and texture. If you can't find either, select mangoes that are fragrant but still firm (but not rock hard). Since the fish is just barely heated through, I suggest you have all the fixings—cabbage, salsa, and avocado—prepped before you grill the fish.

Gently remove the cooked fish fillets from the bag, discarding any liquid in the bag, and transfer it to a plate or tray. Thoroughly pat the fish dry with paper towels. Coat the surface of each piece evenly with the olive oil. Set aside.

MAKE THE SALSA: Stir together the lime juice, red onion, habanero, and a pinch of salt, and toss to coat the onion evenly. While the mixture is marinating, peel the mango. Add the mango and cilantro to the lime-onion mixture, stir to combine, and season to taste with pepper and additional salt. Set aside for up to 1 hour, or up to 24 hours in a tightly sealed container in the fridge.

Sprinkle the avocado with a squeeze of lime juice and the cumin. Set aside.

Preheat a grill pan or skillet over medium-high heat.

Working in batches, heat the tortillas by stacking 2 tortillas sandwiched together directly onto the grill. Leave undisturbed until they begin to steam and blister, and the bottom tortilla begins to char in places, about 30 seconds, then flip them with tongs or a spatula and cook for about another 30 seconds. Depending on the size of your pan, you may be able to fit 2 stacks of tortillas at once. After each stack is heated through, transfer the tortillas to a plate and cover them with a kitchen towel or aluminum foil to keep warm. Set aside.

If the fillets are coming straight from the refrigerator, sear them for a total of 4 to 5 minutes, using a spatula to flip the pieces halfway through, until dark golden-brown grill marks have formed and the pieces are heated through. If using just-cooked fish, cook for only 2 to 3 minutes, flipping halfway through, once the grill marks have formed (don't worry if the fish breaks apart somewhat during cooking) transfer the fish to a bowl or plate.

Place 2 warm tortillas on individual plates, evenly distribute the grilled fish pieces on top (separating into large flakes), and top each taco with the cabbage, avocado, a dollop of mango salsa, a sprinkle of flaky salt, and a few leaves of cilantro. Serve with any additional salsa on the side.

SERVES 4
🕐 **20 MINUTES**

---

1 MASTER RECIPE Flaky White Fish (page 120), just cooked or straight from the fridge

Olive oil, for coating the fish

MANGO SALSA

2 tablespoons fresh lime juice (from about ½ lime)

½ small red onion, thinly sliced

1 ripe habanero or Scotch bonnet chile pepper, stemmed, seeded, and finely minced (see Cooking Tip, facing page), or 1 or 2 red serrano or jalapeño peppers, stemmed, seeded, and chopped

Salt

1 medium or 2 small mangos, ripe but firm, peeled and cut into ¼-inch dice (1½ cups)

¼ cup chopped cilantro

Freshly ground black pepper

FIXINGS

1 ripe avocado, halved, pitted, peeled, and sliced into thin wedges

Squeeze of lime juice

Pinch of ground cumin

12 (6-inch) corn tortillas

1 cup thinly sliced or shredded cabbage

Flaky sea salt, such as Maldon or fleur de sel

2 tablespoons cilantro leaves

FISH CHOWDER

SERVES 4 TO 6

🕐 **25 MINUTES**

1 MASTER RECIPE Flaky White Fish (page 120; preferably cod), just cooked or straight from the fridge

1 teaspoon canola or other neutral vegetable oil

2 or 3 strips bacon (about 3 ounces), finely chopped

1 tablespoon unsalted butter

1 large leek, white and light green parts, halved lengthwise and washed, or 1 large shallot, thinly sliced

1 celery stalk, thinly sliced

1 clove garlic, minced

Salt

¼ cup all-purpose flour

1 (12-ounce) can or bottle of pilsner, or ¾ cup dry white wine or vermouth

1 large russet or 2 Yukon gold potatoes, peeled and cut into ½-inch dice (about 2 cups)

1 cup chicken stock, homemade (page 176) or low-sodium store-bought broth

1 (8-ounce) bottle of clam juice

½ teaspoon chopped fresh thyme, or a pinch of dried thyme

½ cup heavy cream or crème fraîche

1 to 3 teaspoons freshly squeezed lemon juice

Freshly ground white or black pepper

2 tablespoons chopped fresh Italian parsley, for garnish

While my fish chowder isn't a traditional New England–style clam chowder—owing to the lack of Old Bay seasoning, salt pork, and actual clam bellies—the combination of just-poached flaky cod and a cream-enriched clam broth will convert even the most die-hard New Englander. Take it over the top with oyster crackers, fresh rolls, or my Flaky Buttermilk Biscuits (page 175).

While the fish is still in the bag, use your fingertips to gently break apart the fillets into large flakes—they'll break down further when added to the soup. (Any liquid in the bag will be added along with the fish, later.) Set aside.

Heat the oil in a Dutch oven or large pot over medium-high heat until shimmering, then add the bacon. Cook, stirring frequently, until the bacon pieces are crisp, 3 to 4 minutes. Stir in the butter and then add the leek, celery, garlic, and a pinch of salt and cook, stirring occasionally, until the vegetables are translucent and begin to soften (but not brown), 2 to 3 minutes. Add the flour, stirring vigorously to combine, and cook for another 1 minute.

Stir in the beer, bring to a boil, and cook for 2 to 3 minutes, until the liquid has slightly reduced. Stir in the potatoes, chicken stock, clam juice, and thyme and allow the soup to return to a boil. Reduce the heat to a simmer and cook until the potatoes are tender but not falling apart, and the broth is thick enough to coat the back of a spoon, 6 to 10 minutes.

Remove from the heat, stir in the cream and lemon juice to taste, and season to taste with pepper and additional salt (you might not need the latter, as the clam juice has plenty of salt). Stir in the flaked fish, along with any cooking liquid in the bag. If using just-cooked fish, ladle the soup into bowls immediately after stirring in the fish. If you're using fish directly from the fridge, allow the chowder to sit for 2 to 3 minutes to fully reheat the fish before ladling into soup bowls. Garnish with parsley and serve.

It's important to use a Thai brand of tamarind concentrate (also sold as liquid tamarind soup base), because Indian brands are more reduced, resulting in a stronger molasses flavor that doesn't fit this dish.

VIETNAMESE SWEET AND SOUR FISH STEW

The mouthwatering combination of sweet pineapple, tangy tamarind, and aromatic herbs makes for a truly unforgettable fish soup. This is my interpretation of those quintessentially Vietnamese flavors. Born among the rich waterways of the Mekong Delta in Vietnam, where it's known as *canh chua cá*, this dish is traditionally made with freshwater fish such as catfish, but any mild, flaky fish will be delicious. Serve it over bowls of steamed rice to soak up all the flavors.

Heat the oil in a large pot over medium heat. Stir in the garlic and shallot and cook, stirring constantly, until softened and translucent, about 5 minutes. Add the water, sugar, tamarind, and 1 tablespoon of the fish sauce and bring to a boil. Reduce the heat to a simmer and stir in the pineapple and tomato. Continue to simmer until the tomato has begun to soften, but not falling apart, 2 to 3 minutes. Remove from the heat.

While the fish is still in the bag, use your fingertips to gently break apart the fillets into large flakes—they'll break down further when added to the stew. Add the flaked fish to the broth, along with any liquid in the bag, and stir to disperse the fish pieces evenly. Taste for seasoning and add additional fish sauce if desired. If you're using fish directly from the fridge, allow the fish to sit in the hot broth for another 2 to 3 minutes to ensure that it's warmed through completely.

Ladle the soup into bowls and top with the bean sprouts, cilantro, basil, and chiles. Serve immediately.

SERVES 4 TO 6
🕐 **20 MINUTES**

---

1 tablespoon canola or other neutral vegetable oil

2 cloves garlic, minced

2 shallots, thinly sliced

5 cups water

1 tablespoon palm sugar or light brown sugar

¼ cup tamarind juice concentrate (see Shopping Tip, facing page), or 3 tablespoons lime juice mixed with an additional 1 tablespoon palm or light brown sugar

1 to 2 tablespoons fish sauce, as needed

1 cup coarsely chopped fresh pineapple, or 1 (6-ounce) can pineapple juice

2 plum tomatoes, cored, halved lengthwise, and sliced into thin wedges

1 MASTER RECIPE Flaky White Fish (page 120), just cooked or straight from the fridge

1 cup bean sprouts, for garnish

½ cup coarsely chopped cilantro, for garnish

¼ cup regular or Thai basil leaves, for garnish (optional)

1 or 2 red chiles (such as bird, Fresno, or finger), seeded if desired, thinly sliced, for garnish (optional)

VEGETABLES

TIPS FOR SUBMERGING VEGETABLES WITHOUT A VACUUM SEALER

Veggies such as cauliflower and mushrooms are prone to floating because they're less dense than water. So if you plan to cook a lot of veggies sous vide, you might want to invest in a vacuum sealer. You can pick up a fairly inexpensive model, such as FoodSaver, that is adequate for home use at retail warehouses or online for about $150.

That said, if you don't want to invest in a vacuum sealer, the good news is that you can still use sous vide to cook veggies perfectly well in ziplock bags using the water displacement method (page 12); the trick is adding enough weight to the bag (and possibly on top of the bag) to ensure that it sinks and stays fully submerged. Just be sure to dip the bag underwater, remove the air, and seal the bag tightly *before* the water comes up to the targeted temperature; although the water won't be boiling, 85°C (185°F) is still dangerously hot when you attempt to do this with your bare hands. And be sure to remove the bag once it's sealed and wait for the water to reach the target temperature before dropping it back in to start the timed cooking process.

INTERNAL WEIGHTING: To ensure that your bag sinks and stays submerged, add 1 to 2 pounds of weight directly into the bottom of the bag, such as two to four stainless steel spoons or *dull* butter knives. (Avoid using anything sharp to prevent puncturing the bag.) You can also use pie weights, glass marbles, ball bearings, or even freshly scrubbed river rocks; just but be sure to put any object that's not food-grade into its own sealed bag first (getting out as much of the air as possible) before adding it to your bagged food.

EXTERNAL WEIGHTING: If your food still keeps floating above the waterline, try clipping a small bulldog or binder clip to the bottom of the bag to help it sink. Alternatively, you can place something over the bag (such as inverted dinner plate, large heavy bowl, large kitchen tongs, or an expandable stainless steel vegetable steamer placed upside down) over the bag to keep it submerged. Experiment until you find what works.

The only iron-clad rule is that you need to make sure there's still proper hot water circulation above, below, and around the food for the entire duration of cooking, so make sure you're not pinning the bags down to the bottom or flush against the side of your cooking vessel. Inserting a colander or a small rack into the cooking vessel will prevent this.

CHECK ON YOUR BAGS: Keep an eye on the bag during the cooking process. Oftentimes, as the air in the bag heats up, it expands and the bag floats to the top of the water. If this occurs, you may have to reseal the bag, which should help it resink.

ROOT VEGETABLES

When it comes to sous vide, vegetables tend to get short shrift—but as so many of us are trying to eat more healthfully, I think it's high time we change that. My husband and son don't eat meat, so I know all too well the challenge of preparing enticing plant-based meals! The spin-off recipes in this chapter are designed to show you just how easy it is to transform everyday pantry items like humble root vegetables into showstopping dishes such as Tandoori-Style Carrots and Chickpeas (page 138), whether you serve them to complement your main dish or as the star attraction itself.

All the recipes in this section call for cooking at 85°C (185°F). This isn't random—85°C is the temperature at which cellulose, the complex carbohydrate responsible for the vegetable's rigid structure, breaks down. Cooking at this temperature is a failsafe way to ensure that the veggies are firm but still soft and yielding. Cooking vegetables this way also offers some real health benefits. Because they're in sealed bags during the cooking process (as opposed to sitting in a pot of boiling water), you're not only bringing their earthy sweetness to the forefront (the flavor has nowhere to go), but none of their valuable nutrients get tossed down the drain.

Preheat the water bath to 85°C (185°F).

Prep your vegetables for the water bath. If cooking carrots, cut off the stem ends and peel. If the carrots are thicker than 1 inch, halve them lengthwise, cutting through the stem end. If cooking sweet potatoes, peel and cut them lengthwise into planks no more than 1 inch thick. Depending on the size of your sweet potatoes, you may need to turn them on their sides and cut the planks into halves or thirds.

Place the carrots or sweet potatoes into a 1-gallon, freezer-safe ziplock bag or a vacuum seal bag, lightly season with salt, and give the bag a good shake to evenly distribute. Seal the bag using the water displacement method (page 12) or a vacuum sealer, adding weights to the bag as necessary (page 130) to ensure that it sinks.

When the water reaches the target temperature, lower the bagged vegetables in the water bath (making sure the bag is fully submerged) and cook for 1 hour (or up to 2 hours).

Remove the bag from the water bath, transfer it to an ice water bath (page 18), and chill until completely cold, about 30 minutes. Once cooked and chilled, the vegetables can be refrigerated in the bag for up to 2 weeks.

Alternatively, if you plan on using the just-cooked veggies in a spin-off recipe right away, let them rest in the bag for at least 10 minutes or up to 1 hour before proceeding.

COOKING TIP

Although I generally don't recommend adding herbs to your bagged food (see page 10 for an explanation), in the case of hard root vegetables such as sweet potatoes, carrots, and their brethren potatoes and parsnips, there's room for an exception. The reason being that vegetables, unlike meat or seafood, are actually porous to aromatic molecules, so you should feel free to add whatever herbs you like to the bag before cooking. I particularly enjoy the flavor of dill, thyme, and parsley. In the following master recipes, I've purposely left out aromatics, allowing you to take the spin-offs in different directions. So if you want to make a flavorful ready-to-eat veggie side, add whatever flavorings you like—whether they be herbs, spices, flavorful fats like butter or olive oil, or acids like citrus juice.

SHOPPING TIP

This master recipe works particularly well with carrots and sweet potatoes, but you can also follow this template for cooking other root vegetables like yams, beets, and parsnips.

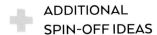

ADDITIONAL SPIN-OFF IDEAS

For a hearty vegetable salad, halve cooked beets lengthwise; dress with a splash of olive oil, vinegar, and orange zest; and top with goat cheese. For the creamiest mashed potatoes you've ever had, add equal parts of cream and butter, along with salt, to a bag of Yukon gold potatoes cut into ½-inch-thick half-moons.

MOROCCAN QUINOA BOWL
WITH GRILLED HARISSA CARROTS

SERVES 4
🕐 **30 MINUTES**

1 MASTER RECIPE Root Vegetables (page 132; made with carrots), just cooked or straight from the fridge

¼ cup harissa, homemade (page 172) or store-bought

3 tablespoons extra-virgin olive oil

1 tablespoon freshly squeezed lemon juice

1 cup quinoa or couscous

1 cup (8 ounces) cherry tomatoes, halved

¼ cup coarsely chopped golden or brown raisins

2 green onions, white and light green parts, thinly sliced

Flaky sea salt, such as Maldon or fleur de sel

¼ cup coarsely chopped or torn fresh mint leaves, for garnish

Harissa is a vibrant, fiery North African condiment often used to enliven couscous. Spiced with red chile along with a typical blend of cumin, caraway, and coriander, it works beautifully with meat, fish, or fowl—but I think it really shines brightest when paired with a sweet vegetable like carrots. This dish is my riff on a Moroccan carrot salad served over couscous, but if you're looking for a more nutrient-dense meal I happen to think that quinoa makes for an equally delicious pairing. Either way, you'll be *bowl*ed over, so feel free to choose your own adventure.

Leaving the cooked carrots in the bag, pour out any cooking liquid into a small bowl and reserve.

In another small bowl, whisk together the harissa, olive oil, and lemon juice to combine. Add 2 tablespoons of the harissa mixture to the bag with the carrots and give it a good shake to make sure the carrots are evenly coated. Set aside to let the carrots soak up all the flavors.

Cook the quinoa according to package instructions, using whatever amount of reserved carrot cooking liquid you have and adding more water or vegetable stock as needed. When the couscous is done, cover and keep warm until you're ready to serve.

Preheat a grill pan or skillet over medium-high heat. Working in batches as necessary, lay the harissa-marinated carrots in a single layer on the grill pan and cook on high for 1 to 2 minutes, until charred in places. Using tongs or a spatula, flip the carrots and cook for 1 to 2 minutes more, then remove from the heat. If you're using cooked carrots straight from the fridge, add an additional 1 to 2 minutes of cooking time to fully reheat, flipping as needed to avoid overbrowning.

Remove the cover from the cooked quinoa and, using two forks, fluff and separate the individual grains. Add 2 tablespoons more of the harissa mixture, along with the cherry tomatoes, raisins, and green onions, and gently fold into the grains using the forks until everything is just combined. Season to taste with the flaky salt.

Divide the finished quinoa mixture between 4 bowls and scatter the grilled carrots on top. Sprinkle with additional flaky salt, if desired, and garnish with the mint. Serve with the remaining harissa mixture on the side.

need all air out of plastic bags — all food must be submerged

SWEET POTATO AND BRUSSELS SPROUT HASH — Time Consuming!

Hash is ready for a renaissance—who says it has to be left in the realm of greasy, meat-loaded diner food? My meatless version is bursting with so much color, flavor, and texture, it's sure to delight vegetarians and carnivores alike. Terrific as a hearty breakfast (for maximum delight, put an egg on it; see page 28) or lunch, it also makes for a light, yet satisfying dinner, especially when accompanied by crusty bread or a side salad. You can easily make this dish vegan by omitting the ricotta, or even Paleo by also leaving out the maple syrup and cooking the veggies in coconut oil instead of canola.

Remove the cooked sweet potatoes from the bag, reserving any liquid in the bag, and cut them into 1-inch chunks. Set aside. Prepare the brussels sprouts by using your fingers to break them apart into leaves.

Heat a large cast-iron skillet over medium-high heat. Add 2 tablespoons of the oil to the pan, heating until shimmering and giving off wisps of smoke. Add the onion and bell pepper and toss to coat. Season with salt and pepper to taste and sauté, stirring frequently, until golden brown and softened, 6 to 8 minutes. Add the brussels sprouts, tossing to incorporate, and cook until wilted, 1 to 2 minutes.

Using a wooden spoon or heat-proof spatula, push the vegetable mixture to the side of the pan, exposing at least half of the bottom of the pan. Add 1 tablespoon more of oil to the exposed pan, followed by the sweet potato. Cook undisturbed for 1 minute, so that the sweet potato begins to brown on the bottom, then toss to combine. Cook 2 to 3 minutes more, tossing or stirring occasionally (being careful not to break up the chunks of sweet potato too much), until the potatoes are deep golden brown in places and fully heated through. If you're using cooked potatoes straight from the fridge, add an additional 1 to 2 minutes of cooking time to fully reheat. *Don't overcook = mushy*

Again using a wooden spoon, push the vegetable mixture to the side to expose a small area of the pan bottom. Add the remaining 1 tablespoon of oil, followed by the garlic and rosemary. Stir the garlic until it begins to turn golden brown, about 1 minute, then toss the mixture to combine. Add the paprika, reserved cooking liquid from the potatoes, the maple syrup, and hot sauce to taste. Cook for 1 to 2 minutes more, until the liquid is almost completely evaporated, then remove from the heat. Add the lemon juice, then adjust seasoning with additional salt and pepper as needed.

Evenly divide the hash among four bowls, and garnish with a dollop of ricotta and a sprinkle each of pecans, parsley, and salt.

SERVES 4
🕐 30 MINUTES

1 MASTER RECIPE Root Vegetables (page 132; made with sweet potato), just cooked or straight from the fridge

4 ounces brussels sprouts, stems ends and tough outer leaves removed, halved (about 1 heaping cup)

4 tablespoons canola or coconut oil

1 yellow onion, cut into ½-inch dice

1 red bell pepper, cut into ½-inch dice

Salt and freshly ground black pepper

3 cloves garlic, thinly sliced *(maybe 5)*

1 teaspoon coarsely chopped rosemary

1 teaspoon smoked paprika

3 tablespoons maple syrup

1 or 2 teaspoons hot sauce

3 tablespoons freshly squeezed lemon or lime juice *(Meyer lemon = best)*

½ cup ricotta cheese

½ cup toasted pecans or walnuts, coarsely chopped

¼ cup chopped parsley, for garnish

Flaky sea salt, such as Maldon or fleur de sel, for garnish

TANDOORI-STYLE CARROTS AND CHICKPEAS

SERVES 4 TO 6

🕐 35 MINUTES

1 MASTER RECIPE Root Vegetables (page 132; made with carrots), just cooked or straight from the fridge

TANDOORI MARINADE

2 tablespoons lemon or lime juice

1 tablespoon peeled and minced fresh ginger, from about 1 (1-inch) piece

3 cloves garlic, minced

Salt

2 tablespoons medium-hot chili powder (such as Kashmiri) or paprika

1 tablespoon tandoori seasoning or garam masala

1 teaspoon ground turmeric

1 teaspoon ground cumin

½ teaspoon ground coriander

¼ to ½ teaspoon cayenne

½ cup plain whole milk yogurt or coconut cream (preferably a Thai brand)

1 teaspoon sugar or honey (optional)

2 tablespoons canola or other neutral vegetable oil

1 red onion, thinly sliced

2 (14- to 16-ounce) cans chickpeas, drained (about 3 cups)

½ cup cilantro, coarsely chopped

4 lemon or lime wedges, for garnish

A tandoor is a clay oven traditionally used for baking the beloved Indian flatbread known as naan. Outside of India, the word *tandoori* is more familiar as a term for a flavorful spiced yogurt marinade used with chicken. For this dish, I decided to apply that delicious marinade to one of India's other beloved staples, the chickpea. Together with sweet carrots, the results are hard to argue with: crispy, creamy, and packed with flavor. After all, what's good for the chicken is good for the chickpea, right? Naan or rice make a delicious accompaniment.

Preheat the oven to 425°F.

Remove the cooked carrots from the bag, reserving any liquid in the bag, and cut them into 2- to 3-inch lengths. Set aside.

MAKE THE TANDOORI MARINADE: In a large nonreactive bowl, mix together the lemon juice, ginger, garlic, and a pinch of salt with a wooden spoon or spatula (first mixing the garlic with the acidic lemon juice will prevent it from becoming overly acrid). Stir in the chili powder, tandoori seasoning, turmeric, cumin, coriander, and cayenne, followed by the yogurt, sugar, and oil, mixing until homogeneous. Season to taste. (The tandoori marinade can be made up to 3 days in advance, stored in an airtight container in the fridge.)

To the same bowl, add the cooked carrots, onion, and chickpeas, tossing until well coated.

Grease a large heatproof baking dish or casserole with oil, then spoon in the carrot chickpea mixture, using a spoon or spatula to spread it into a roughly even layer. Bake for 20 to 25 minutes, until fully heated through and the edges are golden brown (it will be sizzling and some of the chickpeas will have crisped up).

Sprinkle with the cilantro and serve family style or spoon into shallow bowls, with lemon wedges on the side.

In authentic Indian cooking, spice blends are both regional and personal—"curry powder" is a Western bowdlerization of the myriad Indian spice mixes. For this nontraditional Indian-inspired dish, store-bought versions of tandoori seasoning or garam masala will work, though note that no two blends are alike.

SOUS VIDE COOKING TIME
25 minutes (or up to 1 hour)

1 large head cauliflower
(or 2 small heads), about
2½ to 3 pounds

Salt

CAULIFLOWER

Cauliflower's hearty texture makes it a perfect blank canvas, so having bags of perfectly cooked al dente cauliflower steaks on hand is a great strategy for whipping up a substantial vegetarian main course or side dish in a matter of minutes. As with the other vegetables in this section, cooking cauliflower sous vide offers several advantages. Cauliflower in particular has a very short window before turning from raw to mushy. It can also be tricky to cook in a pan without the need to blanch it first or add water to the pan, which prevents browning. The even, precise temperature of a water bath means you'll always end up with tender cauliflower pieces that still hold their shape. This is especially helpful when your recipe calls for twice-cooking the cauliflower as in the case of the flash-fried Manchurian Cauliflower (page 145) and the Greco-inspired grilled Cauliflower Steaks with Kalamata Yogurt Sauce (page 142).

Preheat the water bath to 85°C (185°F).

Prepare the cauliflower by trimming away any outer leaves or discolored stem but leaving the core intact. Place the cauliflower on a cutting board and slice into 1- to 1½-inch-thick slices. Season the cauliflower slices with salt.

Gently transfer the cauliflower into a 1-gallon freezer-safe ziplock bag or a vacuum seal bag, keeping the slices as whole as possible (if they fall apart somewhat, it's okay). Arrange them in a single layer with as little overlap as possible to ensure even cooking.

Seal the bag using the water displacement method (page 12) or a vacuum sealer, adding weights to the bag as necessary (page 130) to ensure that it sinks.

When the water reaches the target temperature, lower the bagged cauliflower in the water bath (making sure the bag is fully submerged) and cook for 25 minutes (or up to 1 hour).

Remove the bag from the water bath, transfer it to an ice water bath (page 18), and chill until completely cold, about 30 minutes. Once cooked and chilled, the cauliflower can be refrigerated in the bag for up to 2 weeks.

Alternatively, if you plan on using the just-cooked cauliflower in a spin-off recipe right away, let it rest in the bag for at least 10 minutes or up to 1 hour before proceeding.

COOKING TIP

If using a particularly large head of cauliflower that makes it too difficult to arrange in a single layer (or if doubling this recipe), use two 1-gallon bags.

ADDITIONAL SPIN-OFF IDEAS

Drizzle the cauliflower florets with lemon juice and capers for a zingy side, toss with penne and Pecorino cheese for a healthy pasta, add at the very last minute to a store-bought curry sauce just heated through, or serve cold with ranch dressing on a crudité platter.

CAULIFLOWER STEAKS
WITH KALAMATA YOGURT SAUCE

SERVES 4

🕐 **20 MINUTES**

KALAMATA YOGURT SAUCE

1 clove garlic, minced or finely grated

1 tablespoon freshly squeezed lemon juice

Salt and freshly ground white or black pepper

½ teaspoon finely grated lemon zest (about ¼ lemon)

1 teaspoon coarsely chopped thyme

1 teaspoon honey

½ cup chopped pitted Kalamata olives, or other ripe olives such as Niçoise

½ cup whole milk Greek yogurt or labneh

4 tablespoons extra-virgin olive oil

1 MASTER RECIPE Cauliflower (page 140), just cooked or straight from the fridge

2 tablespoons unsalted butter

½ cup raw almonds, coarsely chopped

Pinch of red pepper flakes

2 tablespoons crumbled feta, for garnish (optional)

¼ cup coarsely chopped fresh dill, mint, or flat-leaf parsley, or a mix, for garnish

Don't wait till meatless Monday to bust out this recipe. Cauliflower steak may sound like an oxymoron to my carnivore friends, but trust me—one taste of this showstopping vegetarian main course, pan-fried at the last minute in a nutty vinaigrette and slathered with a boldly flavored olive yogurt sauce, and you'll be hooked.

PREPARE THE KALAMATA YOGURT SAUCE: In a medium bowl, combine the garlic, lemon juice, and a pinch of salt and let stand for 5 to 10 minutes to allow the garlic to mellow. Stir in the lemon zest, thyme, honey, olives, yogurt, and 2 tablespoons of the olive oil. Season to taste with pepper. Set aside.

Remove the cooked cauliflower from the bag, discarding any liquid in the bag. Thoroughly pat dry with paper towels.

Line a platter with paper towels and set aside.

In a large skillet or sauté pan, heat the remaining 2 tablespoons of olive oil over medium heat until shimmering. Swirl in the butter (which should immediately sizzle) and cook until it begins to turn golden brown. Carefully lay the cauliflower steaks in the pan in one layer, and sear on both sides until deep golden brown, 6 to 8 minutes total, working in batches if necessary. Lower the heat if browning too quickly.

Remove the pan from the heat and transfer the cauliflower to the paper towel–lined platter, leaving the fat in the pan for the next step. Sprinkle the steaks lightly with salt and set aside.

Return the pan to the heat and add the almonds with a pinch of salt. Toast the nuts, tossing frequently, until they turn light golden brown, 1 to 2 minutes. Stir in the red pepper flakes and remove the pan from the heat.

Dollop the sauce evenly between four individual plates and spread it out with the back of a spoon. Place 1 cauliflower steak on each plate, and then sprinkle the toasted almonds, feta, and herbs evenly over each.

For the sake of health or efficiency, you can skip the steps that call for battering and frying; simply add the chilled cauliflower to the pan after adding the bell pepper to the garlic ginger mixture and cook, stirring frequently, for 2 to 3 minutes, until heated through and beginning to brown. Proceed to add the remaining sauce ingredients, and then toss thoroughly and serve.

Garlic ginger paste, a staple of Indian cuisine, is widely available in Indian and Middle Eastern markets. It can be used in lieu of chopping your own as an additional convenience in this recipe; simply omit the garlic and ginger listed below and use 2 tablespoons of garlic ginger paste instead.

MANCHURIAN CAULIFLOWER

This deep-fried Sino-Indian cauliflower dish similar to America's favorite Chinese takeout staple, General Tso's, arose from Chinese restaurant workers in India adapting to the local palate. If you haven't already cooled the cauliflower in the ice bath, refrigerate for at least 1 hour before frying. This will produce the crispiest, least greasy cauliflower fritters you've ever had.

Remove the cooked cauliflower from the bag using a slotted spoon, discarding any liquid in the bag, and transfer to a plate. Thoroughly pat the cauliflower dry with paper towels. Using a paring knife or just your hands, cut or break the cauliflower into bite-size pieces. Set aside.

Line a baking sheet with paper towels and place near the stove.

Fill a deep-sided skillet or wide Dutch oven with oil to a depth of at least 1½ inches. The oil should come no more than one-third of the way up the side of the skillet to ensure it will not overflow once the cauliflower is added. Heat the oil over medium heat until a wooden skewer or bamboo chopstick inserted into the center of the oil bubbles immediately, or the oil registers 350°F on a high-heat thermometer.

MAKE THE BATTER: While the oil is heating, in a medium bowl, whisk together the flour, cornstarch, and pepper to combine, then add the soy sauce and water; continue whisking until the batter is smooth and the viscosity of thin pancake batter. (If the batter is too thick, add additional water, 1 tablespoon at a time, to thin out.)

Once the frying oil is hot, add the cauliflower to the batter, mixing until the pieces are fully coated. Using your fingers or tongs, lift the coated cauliflower pieces from the batter and transfer them carefully into the hot oil, letting them drop one by one so they don't stick together. Work in batches as necessary to avoid crowding. Fry the cauliflower until golden brown and crisp, 3 to 5 minutes. Transfer the cooked pieces to the paper towel–lined baking sheet and repeat with any remaining pieces.

MAKE THE MANCHURIAN SAUCE: Heat the 2 tablespoons of canola oil in a large wok, skillet, or sauté pan over medium-high heat until shimmering. Add the garlic, ginger, chiles, white and light green parts of the green onion, and bell pepper to the pan and stir-fry until aromatic and beginning to brown, 2 to 3 minutes. Turn the heat to low, add the ketchup, soy sauce, chile paste, and honey to the pan and cook 30 seconds more, until the mixture is quite syrupy.

Remove from the heat, add in the reserved fried cauliflower, and toss until every piece is fully coated. Transfer to a serving bowl or platter, sprinkle with the reserved green onion tops, and serve immediately.

SERVES 4
🕐 **30 MINUTES**

1 MASTER RECIPE Cauliflower (page 140), just cooked and chilled or straight from fridge

2 tablespoons canola or other neutral vegetable oil, plus more for deep-frying

BATTER
½ cup all-purpose flour

¼ cup plus 1 tablespoon cornstarch

1 teaspoon freshly ground black pepper

2 teaspoons soy sauce

½ cup cold water, plus more as needed

MANCHURIAN SAUCE
3 cloves garlic, finely grated or minced

1 tablespoon peeled, minced, or finely grated fresh ginger, from about 1 (1-inch) piece

1 or 2 green chiles (such as serranos or jalapeños), seeded if desired and chopped

4 green onions, white and light green parts, thinly sliced, dark green tops reserved for garnish

1 bell pepper (any color), cut into ½-inch dice

2 tablespoons ketchup

2 tablespoons soy sauce

1 or 2 tablespoons sambal chile paste or Sriracha

1 teaspoon honey (or sugar, if you want it to be vegan)

CAULIFLOWER GRATIN

**SERVES 4 TO 6 AS A MAIN,
6 TO 8 AS A SIDE**

🕐 **40 MINUTES**

1 MASTER RECIPE Cauliflower
(page 140), just cooked or
straight from the fridge

3 tablespoons unsalted butter

1 clove garlic, minced

3 tablespoons all-purpose flour

¼ cup dry white wine

1½ cups whole milk

Pinch of freshly grated nutmeg

½ teaspoon chopped thyme

1½ cup grated Gruyère or
sharp Cheddar

Salt and freshly ground white
pepper

⅓ cup coarse bread crumbs
(such as panko)

Flaky sea salt, such as Maldon or
fleur de sel, for garnish

1 tablespoon chopped fresh
Italian parsley, for garnish

Think of this dish as a slightly healthier potato gratin: all of the creamy, cheesy goodness, but with hearty, nutritious cauliflower filling the lead role. It's wonderful as an indulgent but not-too-guilty weekday meal, accompanied by a nice green salad and crusty bread, but it can also be a luxurious accompaniment to a beef roast or whole roasted chicken.

Preheat the oven to 450°F.

Remove the cooked cauliflower from the bag, discarding any liquid in the bag, and thoroughly pat dry with paper towels. Use a paring knife or just your hands, cut or break the cauliflower into bite-size pieces. Set aside.

Heat 2 tablespoons of the butter in a medium pot over medium-low heat until bubbling. Add the garlic and cook, stirring constantly with a whisk, until fragrant but not browned, about 30 seconds. Add the flour and continue to stir, cooking for 1 minute. Add the wine and then add the milk in a steady stream, whisking constantly to avoid lumps. Increase the heat to medium and bring the sauce to a boil, stirring frequently. Reduce heat to a simmer and cook for 5 minutes, until the sauce is thick enough to coat the back of a spoon.

Remove from the heat and stir in the nutmeg, thyme, and 1 cup of the Gruyère, whisking until smooth. Season to taste with salt and pepper, then stir in the cauliflower to coat.

Lightly grease an 8 by 8-inch baking dish or casserole with butter. Add the cauliflower and sauce mixture and spread it into an even layer with the back of a spoon or spatula. Sprinkle on the remaining ½ cup of Gruyère, followed by the bread crumbs. Dot with the remaining 1 tablespoon of butter, then transfer the dish to the oven. Bake for 20 to 25 minutes, until golden brown and bubbly. Sprinkle with the flaky sea salt and parsley. Let rest for 5 to 10 minutes before serving.

ULTIMATE CORN ON THE COB

SOUS VIDE COOKING TIME

🕐 20 minutes (or up to 40 minutes)

ACTIVE COOKING TIME

🕐 10 minutes

4 ears of corn, shucked

2 tablespoons unsalted butter, melted

Salt

2 tablespoons freshly squeezed lime juice

1 small garlic clove, finely minced

½ cup Mexican-style crema or sour cream

½ cup finely crumbled cotija or queso fresco

½ to 1 tablespoon ancho, guajillo, or other mild or hot ground chile, or 2 teaspoons paprika mixed with 1 teaspoon cayenne

¼ cup chopped cilantro

Cooking corn sous vide, rather than in a pot of water, maximizes the sweet corn flavor (it's got nowhere to go!), and it also makes for the juiciest, just-tender kernel. As a major bonus, because the ears are cooked directly in the butter, this technique lets the butter work its way into the corn's nooks and crannies so you get the most bang for your butter (or buck). This is my version of *elote*, or Mexican grilled corn on the cob. The appeal of this popular street food isn't hard to see (or taste)—sweet corn, salty cheese, tangy sour cream and lime, and an enticing spark of heat from ground chili.

Preheat the water bath to 85°C (185°F).

Place the ears of corn in a 1-gallon freezer-safe ziplock bag or a vacuum seal bag, followed by the melted butter and salt to taste. Toss the corn to coat evenly. Seal the bag using the water displacement method (page 12) or a vacuum sealer, adding weights to the bag as necessary (page 130) to ensure that it sinks.

When the water has reached the target temperature, submerge the bagged corn in the water bath (making sure the bag is fully submerged) and cook for 20 minutes (or up to 40 minutes).

Remove the bag from the water bath, transfer it to an ice water bath (page 24), and chill until completely cold, about 20 minutes. Once cooked and chilled, the corn can be refrigerated in the bag for up to 2 weeks.

If you plan on using the just-cooked corn right away, let it rest in the bag at room temperature for 10 minutes or up to 1 hour before proceeding.

In a shallow bowl large enough to fit an ear of corn, whisk together the lime juice, garlic, and crema. Set aside. Sprinkle the cotija on a plate; set aside.

Preheat a grill pan or cast-iron skillet over high heat.

Remove the ears of corn from the bag, discarding any liquid in the bag, and place on the grill. Grill the corn, rotating it a quarter-turn every 1 minute or so, until it is lightly charred on all sides, about 4 to 5 minutes. (If you are charring corn from the fridge, you may need to add an additional 2 to 3 minutes grilling time.)

As soon as the ears of corn are charred, remove them from the grill and transfer into the bowl with the crema mixture, rotating them to coat evenly. Transfer the ears to the plate of cotija, once again rotating them to coat (the cheese will adhere to the warm crema).

Transfer the coated ears of corn to a serving platter, then sprinkle with the ground chili and chopped cilantro. Serve immediately.

I have photographer Monica Lo to thank for introducing me to another outrageously delicious variation and beloved street food—Taiwanese corn on the cob. To make her version, add to the bag 3 tablespoons soy sauce, 1 tablespoon sugar, and 2 to 3 tablespoons garlic chile paste or Sriracha; include the melted butter but omit the salt; follow the same instructions for cooking and grilling; then finish by garnishing with finely sliced green onions.

If you have perfectly sweet, peak-season corn, sometimes simplicity is the best approach—just follow the instructions to the left to add the ears, butter, and salt in the bag and serve it right out of the water bath, with additional melted butter as desired.

SOUS VIDE COOKING TIME

15 minutes (or up to 30 minutes)

---

1 pound king trumpet, portobello, maitake, or cremini mushrooms

2 tablespoons soy sauce

Pinch of salt

1 or 2 sprigs of fresh herbs (such as thyme, rosemary, or oregano; optional)

MUSHROOMS

My approach to cooking mushrooms is a winner for a number of reasons. It not only draws moisture out of mushrooms, making them brown better in a final cooking step, but it also essentially works as a fast marinade, fully seasoning and infusing them with an additional oomph of umami from the soy (umamoomph?), amping up their inherent "mushroominess." Because sous vide also helps a very perishable ingredient keep longer in your fridge without risk of sudden spoilage—cleaned, cooked, and flavorful, these mushrooms are ready to go on your time, without fear of slime or mold. Be sure to hold onto the reserved cooking liquid in the bag, though; if I don't explicitly instruct you to incorporate it into a sauce in a spin-off dish, as I do with the Balsamic Teriyaki Mushroom Skewers (page 152), it can be saved in an airtight container for 1 week, and added to give a big punch of flavor to your own soups, braises, and sauces.

Preheat the water bath to 85°C (185°F).

Prepare the mushrooms by trimming off the woody stem ends (in the case of the portobellos, just snap off and discard the stems). If your mushrooms have any dirt on them, clean them by rinsing quickly under cold running water or wiping them off with a damp cloth. If using portobellos, leave them whole. For king trumpets, halve larger mushrooms lengthwise, then cut into large bite-size pieces. For the maitakes, gently pull apart or slice into large, bite-size pieces. Creminis can be left whole.

To ensure that your bag sinks, place 1 to 2 pounds of weights (page 130) into a 1-gallon freezer-safe ziplock bag or a vacuum seal bag. Add the mushrooms, soy sauce, and salt and toss lightly to coat the mushrooms evenly. Arrange the mushrooms in a single layer with as little overlap as possible to ensure even cooking.

Seal the bag using the water displacement method (page 12) or a vacuum sealer, adding more weights to the bag as necessary to ensure that it sinks.

When the water reaches the target temperature, lower the bagged mushrooms in the water bath (making sure the bag is fully submerged) and cook for 15 minutes (or up to 30 minutes).

Remove the bag from the water bath, transfer it to an ice water bath (page 18, and chill until completely cold, about 10 minutes. Once cooked and chilled, the mushrooms can be refrigerated in the bag for up to 1 week.

Alternatively, if you plan on using the just-cooked mushrooms in a spin-off recipe right away, let them rest in the bag at room temperature for at least 10 minutes or up to 1 hour before proceeding.

COOKING TIP

Mushrooms, by their very nature, are not as dense as meats or even other vegetables such as carrots, so they're more prone to float in a water bath. If you have a vacuum sealer, now's the time to use it. No sealer? Fear not, the water displacement method works just fine! Simply play around with adding enough weight to the bottom of the ziplock bag (and if necessary, something on top of it) to ensure that it sinks and stays submerged (see page 130).

SHOPPING TIP

The wide world of mushrooms becomes more widely available in grocery stores with every passing year, and this master recipe will work with any sort—but I selected ones that show off the best texture and richest taste: king trumpets, whose large meaty stems make them perfect for grilling; maitakes ("dancing mushroom" in Japanese), also known as hen of the woods, whose frilly edges crisp up nicely on top of my whole wheat pizza; and portobellos, whose large caps are ready-made for sandwiches like a Mexican mushroom torta. If you can't find these varieties, the more ubiquitous cremini—which actually is a baby portobello—will also work.

ADDITIONAL SPIN-OFF IDEAS

Coarsely chop the mushrooms and stir into risotto along with the cooking liquid before adding cheese, sauté with garlic and olive oil to make a simple pasta sauce (adding a little of the cooking liquid as needed to thin the sauce), or sauté with shallots and finish with a splash of heavy cream or dollop of crème fraîche for a simple side dish.

BALSAMIC TERIYAKI MUSHROOM SKEWERS

**SERVES 4 AS A MAIN
COURSE WITH SIDES OR
4 TO 6 AS AN APPETIZER**
🕐 **15 MINUTES**

1 MASTER RECIPE Mushrooms
(page 150; made with creminis
or king trumpets), just cooked
or straight from the fridge

BALSAMIC TERIYAKI GLAZE

1 tablespoon olive oil

2 cloves garlic, minced

1 teaspoon peeled, minced
fresh ginger

¼ cup balsamic vinegar

¼ cup honey

1 tablespoon soy sauce

Freshly ground black pepper

1 green onion, white and green
parts, thinly sliced, for garnish

East meets West with these grilled mushrooms. They make an impressive appetizer or side dish for your next cookout, and they are hearty enough for an easy vegetarian main course served over rice, polenta, shredded cabbage, or salad greens. Cooking them sous vide in a flavorful marinade gives the mushrooms a particularly meaty flavor and texture and prevents them from drying out, which tends to happen when you grill raw mushrooms. Even better, the umami-rich liquid that collects in the bag while cooking becomes the basis for a delicious balsamic teriyaki glaze, so all you need to do is sear the mushrooms in a hot grill pan just before serving.

Line a plate or tray with paper towels.

Remove the cooked mushrooms from the bag, reserving any liquid in the bag, and transfer them to the paper towel–lined plate or tray.

MAKE THE GLAZE: In a small saucepan, heat the oil over medium heat until shimmering. Add the garlic and ginger and cook, stirring constantly, for 1 minute, until aromatic but not browned. Add the reserved mushroom cooking liquid to the pot along with the balsamic, honey, and soy sauce and bring the mixture to a simmer. Cook until the liquid has reduced in volume by two-thirds and is glossy and syrupy and coats the back of a spoon, 5 to 7 minutes. Remove from the heat and add black pepper to taste. Set aside.

Thread the mushrooms lengthwise onto 8 wooden or metal skewers (2 or 3 mushrooms per skewer). Generously brush both sides with the glaze, reserving the remaining glaze to use later.

Heat a grill pan over medium-high heat. Lightly grease the grill pan with olive oil, place the skewers in the pan, and sear the mushrooms until they are well caramelized and crisp on the edges, flipping every 1 minute and brushing with additional glaze as you do so, for a total of 3 to 4 minutes. (If cooking the mushrooms straight from the fridge, you may need to add an additional 1 or 2 minutes of grilling time to ensure they're fully heated through.)

Transfer the grilled mushrooms to a serving platter, brush or drizzle on any remaining glaze, sprinkle with green onions, and serve immediately.

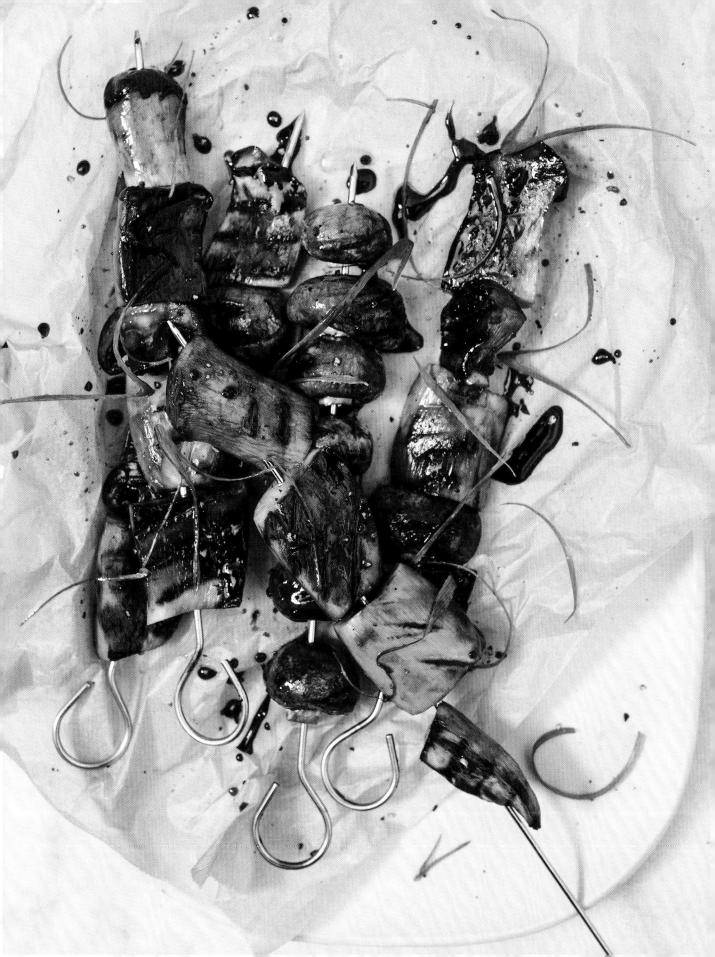

MUSHROOM AND GOAT CHEESE PIZZA

If you like mushrooms, you're gonna love this earthy pizza. I particularly love maitakes (hen of the woods) as a pizza topping because, when roasted, their edges take on a crispy texture—an effect that's enhanced further when you sous vide them beforehand to draw out moisture. That said, any of your favorite mushrooms, even regular ol' buttons, will benefit from the flavor and texture boost offered by cooking them sous vide.

While I'm not going to judge if you reach for store-bought pizza dough, I strongly encourage you to try making your own dough at *yeast* (pun intended) once. My fail-proof recipe comes together in the time it takes you to preheat the oven and, I promise you, the taste of homemade will truly elevate your pizza night.

Preheat the oven to 450°F. Place an inverted baking sheet or a pizza stone in the oven. Line a plate with paper towels.

Remove the cooked mushrooms from the bag, reserving any liquid in the bag for another use, and transfer them to the paper towel–lined plate. Set aside.

Remove the pizza dough from the refrigerator. Dust it with flour and turn it out onto a lightly floured work surface. Gently flatten and spread out the dough with the heel of your hands and then roll it out with a floured rolling pin (or cylindrical wine bottle) until it's approximately ¼ inch thick and fits the size of your baking sheet. (The thinner it is, the crispier the end result will be.) Line a pizza peel or cutting board with parchment paper and grease it with 1 tablespoon of the olive oil. Working your hands under the rolled dough, carefully lift it and transfer to the oiled parchment paper. (Alternatively, if you don't have parchment paper, simply grease a second baking sheet directly with olive oil, then transfer the rolled-out dough onto it and assemble the pizza there.)

Sprinkle the ¼ cup of Parmesan evenly over the surface of the dough and scatter the sliced shallots on top. Break the maitakes into smaller pieces and distribute them evenly in a single layer on top, crumble the goat cheese all over, and drizzle the remaining 1 tablespoon of olive oil evenly over the top. Slip the parchment and pizza onto the preheated inverted baking sheet or pizza stone.

Place the pizza in the oven and cook for 25 to 30 minutes, until the edges of the crust, cheese, and mushrooms are deep golden brown and crisped, rotating the parchment (or pan) as necessary so that it cooks evenly. Remove from the oven and transfer to a cutting board. Sprinkle with the red pepper flakes, thyme, arugula, and additional Parmesan and serve immediately. Pizza party!

SERVES 4 TO 8

🕐 **35 MINUTES (PLUS 50 MINUTES IF MAKING YOUR OWN PIZZA DOUGH)**

---

1 MASTER RECIPE Mushrooms (page 150; made with maitakes), just cooked or straight from the fridge

1 recipe Whole Wheat Pizza Dough (page 174) or 1 pound store-bought dough, straight from the fridge

2 tablespoons extra-virgin olive oil

¼ cup finely grated Parmesan (preferably Parmigiano-Reggiano), plus more for garnish

1 shallot, thinly sliced

8 ounces fresh goat cheese

Pinch of red pepper flakes

1 teaspoon fresh thyme or oregano leaves, or ¼ teaspoon dried

¼ cup fresh arugula or baby spinach (optional), for garnish

PORTOBELLO MUSHROOM TORTA

SERVES 4
🕐 **10 MINUTES**

1 MASTER RECIPE Mushrooms (page 150; made with 4 very large portobellos or 8 small ones, stemmed), just cooked or straight from the fridge

1 clove garlic, finely minced

½ teaspoon ground cumin

1 tablespoon canola or other neutral vegetable oil

4 Mexican *bolillos* (traditional small crusty loaves of white bread) or any large crusty roll, halved (toasted if desired)

1 ripe avocado, halved, pitted, peeled, and cut into ¼-inch slices

Juice of ½ lime, about 1 tablespoon

½ cup salsa roja, homemade (page 171) or store-bought

¼ cup grated or finely crumbled cotija, aged jack, or other salty crumbly cheese

¼ cup cilantro leaves

1 jalapeño, seeded if desired, thinly sliced

Is it portabella or portobello? You'll see lots of variant spellings of this now-familiar mushroom, which came into vogue in the 1980s as a novel way to sell what turns out to be nothing more than a fully matured cremini. By any name, the large meaty caps of these mushrooms make them an ideal sandwich filling. This recipe is my take on the Mexican torta, complementing the portobello's meaty texture with creamy avocado, bright salsa roja, and salty cotija cheese. The tortas work best with four very large portobello caps, but it's fine to double up if you can only find smaller ones.

Remove the cooked mushrooms from their bag, reserving any liquid in the bag. Transfer the mushrooms to a plate or tray and rub with the garlic, cumin, and oil to coat evenly.

Preheat a large cast-iron skillet over medium-high heat. Sear the mushrooms until golden brown, 1 to 2 minutes per side. Remove the pan from the heat.

If toasting the rolls, do so now.

ASSEMBLE THE TORTAS: Divide the avocado slices among the bottom halves of the 4 rolls, sprinkle lime juice on top, and top with the seared mushrooms (doubling up if using small ones). Generously spoon the salsa roja on top of the mushrooms; sprinkle with the cheese, cilantro, and sliced jalapeño; and close up the sandwiches with the roll tops. Serve immediately.

DESSERTS

6 egg yolks

¾ cup sugar

1 tablespoon honey or
light corn syrup

1 teaspoon vanilla extract or seeds
scraped from 1 vanilla pod

Pinch of salt

3 cups half-and-half, or
1½ cup whole milk and
1½ cup heavy cream

Additional flavors and/or mix-ins
(see Additional Custard Flavors to
Try, facing page; optional)

ICE CREAM AND CUSTARD BASE

The following recipe yields a basic vanilla custard, but you can easily transform it with your favorite flavors by simply stirring in your choice of ingredients to the bag of cooked custard before chilling it (see Additional Custard Flavors to Try, facing page, for some of my favorite variations). This one master recipe can be churned into ice cream, layered with fruit and cake to make parfaits, or used to make the base of a pie filling before freezing.

The key to making smooth, creamy custard is to thicken it without curdling. Conventional techniques attempt this by heating the egg mixture gradually and often call for tempering the eggs and using a double boiler—but honestly, who wants to have to babysit a pot just to make an everyday treat? Sous vide is tailor-made for this purpose since it allows you to cook custards below the point at which yolks curdle (85°C/185°F), so you'll hit the mark every time. No more crying over curdled milk!

Preheat the water bath to 83°C (181.4°F).

In a large bowl, whisk together the egg yolks, sugar, honey, vanilla, and salt. Add the half-and-half and whisk until combined. Pour the custard base into a 1-gallon, freezer-safe zip bag and seal using the table-edge method (see page 13).

When the water has reached the target temperature, lower the bagged custard in the water bath (making sure the bag is fully submerged). After 15 minutes, carefully remove the bag from the water bath and transfer it to a flat surface. Massage the contents of the bag with your fingertips to "stir" the custard (covering the bag with a kitchen towel if necessary to avoid burning your fingers). This will help the curds form more evenly, resulting in the smoothest custard. Return the bag to the water bath. Repeat the massaging step at 15-minute intervals three more times (for a total of 1 hour cooking time), but do not return the bag to the bath after the last massage.

If you plan to make ice cream and want something other than vanilla, now's the time to add a flavoring to the custard. While the custard is still hot, carefully open the bag (or set inside a bowl, if you're worried about spilling), add your extra ingredients, and reseal the bag. Massage the contents using your fingertips until thoroughly combined (covering the bag with a kitchen towel if necessary to avoid burning your fingers). Alternatively, pour the hot custard into a bowl and whisk in the mix-in to combine before returning to the bag.

Transfer the custard bag to an ice water bath (see page 18) and chill for at least 45 minutes, or refrigerate the bag for least 6 hours. Either way, the custard needs to be fully chilled before freezing to yield the smoothest results. Once chilled, the custard is ready to be used in any of the spin-off recipes or spun into ice cream. Left sealed in the fridge, the custard will last for up to 1 week.

TO MAKE ICE CREAM: Freeze the custard base in an ice cream machine according to the manufacturer's instructions or freeze without an ice cream machine as directed in the box at right. Transfer the frozen custard base into an airtight freezer-safe container and store in the freezer for up to 1 week. Homemade ice cream lacks the stabilizers used in many commercial varieties, so for the very best texture, I don't recommend storing for longer than that.

ADDITIONAL CUSTARD FLAVORS TO TRY

CHOCOLATE: Make a chocolate sauce by combining ¼ cup cocoa powder (natural or Dutch-processed), ¼ cup sugar, and ¼ cup boiling water in a small bowl, whisking until completely smooth. Alternatively, use ½ cup store-bought chocolate sauce or fudge sauce.

CARAMEL: ½ cup store-bought caramel sauce or dulce de leche.

NUT: ⅓ cup smooth peanut butter, almond butter, or other nut butter. (For the best texture, I prefer creamy processed peanut butter—Skippy for life, yo). For a more intense flavor, add 1 or 2 drops of almond or hazelnut extract, or up to 1 teaspoon of amaretto, Frangelico, or other nut-flavored liqueur, if desired.

FRUIT: ½ cup jam, jelly, or marmalade, pressed through a strainer, if desired, for smoothest texture. For a more intense flavor, add a few drops of fruit extract (such as orange or lemon) or up to 1 teaspoon of fruit liqueur, if desired.

If you want to add additional mix-ins to your ice cream, such as chopped nuts for crunch or a swirl of caramel, fold or stir them in once the ice cream is just frozen, but before storing it in the freezer. If you want to see your mix-ins as swirls in the final ice cream, mix just once or twice to distribute.

HOW TO FREEZE WITHOUT AN ICE CREAM MACHINE

In a large container, mix together 1 pound of salt and 3 quarts of warm water, stirring until the salt completely dissolves. Split the brine equally between two 1-gallon zip bags. Lay the bags flat in the freezer and freeze overnight.

Lay a kitchen towel down on the counter and sandwich your bagged custard base between the two bags of frozen brine. Cover the bags with one or two more kitchen towels to insulate. Let the bags sit, covered, for 30 to 40 minutes, or until frozen but still malleable. If desired, transfer the ice cream into a freezer-safe container for easier scooping. Store for up to 1 week for best texture. (You can save the bagged brine in the freezer for the next time you make ice cream.)

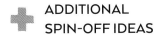

ADDITIONAL SPIN-OFF IDEAS

Left chilled and unfrozen, this custard is delicious as *crème anglaise*, an extremely versatile sauce widely used in classic French desserts. Or fold in whipped cream and freeze until firm to make semifreddo, a classic Italian dessert akin to frozen mousse.

DREAMY ICE CREAM SANDWICHES

MAKES 6 ICE CREAM SANDWICHES

🕐 **40 MINUTES**

1 MASTER RECIPE Ice Cream and Custard Base (page 160; made with any flavor you like), frozen in an ice cream machine according to the manufacturer's instructions

BUTTER COOKIES

½ cup unsalted butter, at room temperature

¾ cup sugar

¼ cup honey or light corn syrup

1 large egg

1 teaspoon vanilla extract

1¾ cups all-purpose flour

2 tablespoons cornstarch

¾ teaspoon salt

½ teaspoon baking powder

Ice cream sandwiches always bring back warm (or should that be cool?) childhood memories of the Good Humor truck. I'm fond of using orange ice cream (made with orange marmalade) to replicate the classic Creamsicle, or peanut butter ice cream for a Nutter Butter flavor, but there's no reason to limit yourself to just those two options. Since we're all grown-ups now, I encourage you to make these ice cream sandwiches from scratch using my delicious yet simple butter cookies. The honey and cornstarch make them especially tender—ideal for sandwiching. If you don't have the time to bake your own cookies, use any type of store-bought cookies you like, from snickerdoodles to chocolate chip—just bear in mind that softer cookies work best if you don't want the ice cream to squeeze out when you bite. To make this a truly quick-to-throw-together dessert, make the ice cream and bake the cookies ahead of time, but resist the urge to assemble the ice cream sandwiches in advance: they're easiest to eat, and the texture is best, when the cookies are room temp and the ice cream is frozen solid.

Preheat the oven to 350°F. Line two baking sheets with parchment paper or a silicone baking mat and set aside.

READY THE ICE CREAM FILLING: Line another baking sheet with parchment. Use an ice cream scoop to divide the frozen custard into 6 large scoops and place them on the tray. Flatten each scoop slightly before returning the ice cream to the freezer for at least 30 minutes, until it's firm again.

MAKE THE COOKIES: In a large bowl, combine the butter, sugar, and honey and, using a wooden spoon or a hand mixer, beat together until smooth and fluffy. Add the egg and vanilla extract and stir until combined. Add the flour, cornstarch, salt, and baking powder and mix until they're just incorporated. (At this point, the dough can be covered and refrigerated for up to 1 week before baking). Using a 2-ounce cookie scoop or two large spoons, scoop the dough into twelve equal mounds. Arrange the dough mounds between the two prepared baking sheets, leaving at least 2 inches between each mound.

Place the baking sheets in the oven and bake for 12 to 14 minutes, until the cookies have spread and the tops are set, but not browned, rotating as necessary for even baking. Transfer the baked cookies to a wire rack and let cool completely before using. (Once cooled, the cookies can be stored in an airtight container for up to 1 week at room temperature.)

When you're ready to serve, place 6 cookies, flat side up, on a serving tray. Transfer the ice cream scoops onto the cookies using an offset spatula, then place the remaining 6 cookies, flat side down, on top of the ice cream to close the sandwiches, pressing down firmly so they stick.

CHOCOLATE RASPBERRY PARFAITS

Chilled custard can be used to make one of the easiest desserts around: parfaits. I love the interplay of chocolate custard, fresh raspberries, and vanilla cake, but this recipe works beautifully for whatever flavor combinations you want to dream up (see page 161). For the tastiest results, I like to chill the assembled parfait glasses in the fridge for at least 1 hour, or up to 24 hours, to give the cake time to soak up the custard, but it's awfully delicious right after assembly. Either way, it's simply parfait!

While no one ever complained about having too much dessert, do note that a full master recipe of my ice cream and custard base makes enough for 8 servings of parfait. So feel free to cut this recipe in half and store the second half of the custard in the fridge to use another time.

In a large bowl, whip the heavy cream and framboise together until stiff peaks are formed.

For the prettiest results, you want clearly distinct layers of custard and cake. The easiest way to achieve this is to turn the bag the custard was cooked in into a pastry bag by snipping off a corner of the bag, so you can pipe it carefully into the glasses.

Divide half of the cake cubes among eight parfait glasses (any glass serving cups or ramekins around 12 ounces in size will work). Pour or pipe half of the chilled custard on top of the cake cubes, doing your best to avoid pouring the custard on the sides of the glasses. Top with a dollop of the whipped cream per glass, using up half the cream in the process, and using the back of a spoon to smooth it out into a somewhat even layer. Sprinkle half the raspberries among the glasses. Repeat the layers with the remaining cake cubes, custard, whipped cream, and raspberries. Place the parfait glasses in the fridge for at least 1 hour (or up to 24 hours) or grab a spoon and dive right in. Just before serving, garnish the glasses with a sprinkle of shaved chocolate.

SERVES 8
🕐 **5 MINUTES, PLUS 1 HOUR TO CHILL**

2 cups heavy cream

2 tablespoons framboise or other raspberry liqueur (optional)

4 cups cubed pound cake or angel food cake store-bought (½-inch cubes)

1 MASTER RECIPE Ice Cream and Custard Base (page 160; made with chocolate), chilled but not frozen

1 pint raspberries

2 ounces bittersweet chocolate, shaved with a box grater or vegetable peeler (about ½ cup), for garnish

---

To serve this family-style, assemble the ingredients into a large dish (such as a 4-quart cake pan, trifle dish, or glass bowl) and voilà, you've got what the British call trifle. To make tiramisu trifle, use vanilla custard base in place of chocolate, replace the heavy cream with mascarpone, substitute rum or brandy in place of framboise, and omit the raspberries. Before assembling, sprinkle the cake cubes with ¼ cup espresso or strong coffee and ¼ cup marsala wine before layering. Chill for at least 1 hour before serving.

FROZEN KEY LIME PIE

Who doesn't love the bright, citrusy flavor of key lime pie? The *key* in the name refers to the Florida Keys, where this petite variety (also called a Mexican lime) is widely found. These limes are more tart and aromatic than their larger cousins, making them ideal for an extra-tangy dessert, but standard limes will still be delicious. Making my graham cracker crust is dead simple, but if you're pressed for time, I give you permission to use a store-bought one.

SERVES 6 TO 8

🕐 **4 HOURS**

GRAHAM CRACKER CRUST

1½ cups graham cracker or gingerbread crumbs

6 tablespoons unsalted butter, melted

3 tablespoons sugar

Pinch of salt (optional)

FILLING

1 cup heavy cream, cold

1 (14-ounce) can sweetened condensed milk, cold

½ cup freshly squeezed lime juice (preferably from key limes)

1 tablespoon finely grated lime zest (preferably from key limes), plus more for garnish

1 MASTER RECIPE Ice Cream and Custard Base (page 160), chilled but not frozen

Preheat the oven to 375°F.

MAKE THE CRUST: Combine the graham cracker crumbs, butter, and sugar in a medium bowl, mixing until the crumbs are evenly coated with the butter. Using your hands or the back of a spoon or spatula, press the crumb mixture into a 9-inch pie plate to form an even crust about ¼ inch thick. Bake for 10 to 12 minutes, until the crust has taken on a darker shade of brown. Transfer the pie dish to a rack to cool. Once cool, the crust can be tightly wrapped in plastic wrap and stored in the freezer for up to 1 month.

MAKE THE FILLING: In a large bowl, whisk together the cream with ¼ cup of the condensed milk and beat together until stiff peaks are formed. In a separate bowl, whisk together the remaining condensed milk with the lime juice and zest, until smooth. Add the chilled custard base and whisk until smooth. Add half of the whipped cream to the custard mixture and whisk until incorporated. Add the second half of the whipped cream, now using a rubber spatula to gently fold it in until just combined, and no streaks of white remain (the goal is to keep the whipped cream as aerated as possible).

Pour the filling into the prepared graham cracker crust and, using the spatula or the back of a spoon, smooth the top. Transfer the pie to the freezer to chill for at least 3 hours, or until completely firm.

When you're ready to serve, remove the pie from the freezer, dip a knife into very hot water and wipe dry with a towel before cutting, repeating until the pie is cut into the desired number of slices. Transfer to serving plates, and garnish with additional lime zest and a dollop of whipped cream, if desired.

🥄 For a show-stopping dessert, turn this into a Baked Key West, my sun-kissed version of a Baked Alaska. Up to 1 hour before serving, make a meringue: whisk together 6 egg whites and a pinch of cream of tartar until foamy, gradually add 1 cup sugar, and beat until the mixture is glossy and stiff peaks have formed. Remove the pie from the freezer, spoon the meringue over the top to completely cover the filling, and brown under a broiler set to high.

PANTRY

BASICS, SAUCES, AND CONDIMENTS

When it comes to everyday cooking, convenience is key. I don't expect you to cap off a busy day whipping up a batch of buttermilk biscuits or grinding your own spice mix, so if a good ready-made alternative is available, I give you my blessing to use it.

As for best condiments, baked goods, and other essentials to have on hand, I think there's something deeply satisfying about making your own. I've included some of my tried-and-true favorites in this section. These recipes are easy to make and can be prepared in advance, yet undoubtedly produce superior results to store-bought versions. So whenever you're feeling like you have a little extra time in the kitchen, I encourage you to give these a shot. There's no need to fire up your immersion circulator though—these recipes call for conventional cooking methods. The only bath required is a relaxing one at the end of the night.

SALSA ROJA

Along with its counterpart, salsa verde, this versatile spicy red sauce, made from tomatoes (as opposed to green tomatillos), is used in Mexican cuisine to enliven everything from enchiladas and carne asada to a Mexican torta (page 156). While we all have our favorite store-bought and taqueria versions, making your own salsa is a snap—and this recipe can easily be doubled so you always have salsa on hand. If you prefer a mild salsa, use the smallest amount of chiles and remove the seeds.

Heat the oil in a small pan over medium-low heat until shimmering, then add the garlic and cook for 1 to 2 minutes, stirring constantly, until the garlic is light golden brown and very fragrant.

Add the chiles and cook, stirring constantly, for 1 to 2 minutes, until the chiles begin to turn a lighter color and become very fragrant. Stir in the chipotle, followed by the tomato puree, and cook for 2 to 3 minutes, stirring occasionally, until the mixture is reduced to a thick paste. Add the water, bring the mixture to a boil, and cook for 1 minute more. Cover and remove from the heat and let cool slightly. Transfer the mixture to a blender or food processor and blend into a course puree. Use right away or let cool completely before transferring to an airtight container. The salsa can be stored in the fridge for up to 2 weeks.

MAKES 2 CUPS

2 tablespoons canola or other neutral vegetable oil

3 cloves garlic, peeled, lightly smashed with the side of a knife

3 or 4 guajillo, ancho, or pasilla chiles, stemmed, seeded, and cut into ¼-inch strips

1 canned chipotle in adobo, seeded if desired

1 cup tomato puree

1 cup water

SSAMJANG

This deeply flavored, sweet and spicy Korean condiment—which gets its name from *ssam*, which means "wrapped" and *jang*, meaning "sauce"— is served with grilled dishes like *bulgogi* (barbecued beef) or pork belly, wrapped with rice in lettuce leaves. The main ingredient, doenjang, is a Korean slow-fermented soybean paste similar to Japanese miso, which is readily available in Asian markets and online. Once you've tried ssamjang on my Korean BBQ-Style Steak (page 84), I have no doubt you'll find infinite ways to weave this addictive, umami-rich sauce into your everyday meals.

In a small nonreactive bowl, mix all of the ingredients until thoroughly combined. The mixture can be stored in an airtight container in the refrigerator for up to 1 month.

MAKES ABOUT ½ CUP

¼ cup doenjang or white miso

2 tablespoons gochujang, or an additional 1 tablespoon doenjang or white miso and 1 tablespoon Sriracha

2 teaspoons honey or light brown sugar

1 green onion, white and green parts, finely chopped

1 clove garlic, minced

2 teaspoons toasted sesame seeds

2 teaspoons toasted sesame oil

HARISSA

This irresistible North African hot sauce made from chiles, garlic, and toasted seeds is as versatile as it is delicious. Store-bought versions, available in jars, cans, or tubes, abound and vary in heat, but my version hits just the right notes. Its tangy, smoky, spiced flavors make it a perfect condiment for perking up grilled or roasted vegetables like the carrots in my Moroccan Quinoa Bowl (page 134), slathering on meats and fish, stirring into stews, or using anywhere you'd use a hot sauce.

MAKES ABOUT ¾ CUP

1 teaspoon caraway seeds

1 teaspoon cumin seeds

½ teaspoon coriander seeds

2 cloves garlic, minced

½ teaspoon salt

1 tablespoon apple cider vinegar, wine vinegar, or lemon juice

½ cup (2 ounces) Aleppo, Espelette, or other moderately hot red pepper flakes

¼ cup extra-virgin olive oil

Preheat a small pan over medium heat. Add the caraway, cumin, and coriander seeds and toast, tossing frequently until aromatic and beginning to brown (they will pop in the pan), 30 seconds to 1 minute. Transfer the toasted spices to the bowl of a mortar and pestle or spice grinder and let cool completely, 1 to 2 minutes, before grinding them as finely as possible.

Using the edge of a knife blade on a cutting board, crush the garlic with the salt to form a paste. Transfer to a small bowl and whisk together with vinegar. Mix in the ground seeds, pepper flakes, and olive oil, whisking vigorously until everything is thoroughly combined. The mixture can be stored in an airtight container in the refrigerator for up to 1 month.

NO-WHISK HOMEMADE MAYONNAISE

When it comes to flavor, homemade mayonnaise handily beats any store-bought version. But I know what you're thinking—who has the time (and forearm strength) to be hunched over a mixing bowl, endlessly whisking? Don't worry, I've got your back. This recipe relies on a blender or food processor to do the emulsifying step—no heavy lifting here. Use this mayo to make an extra-creamy herbed aioli for the Pork Belly BLT (page 70), upgrade your coleslaw, or slather on your favorite sandwiches.

MAKES ABOUT 1½ CUPS

1 raw egg

2 teaspoons Dijon mustard

2 teaspoons freshly squeezed lemon juice or apple cider vinegar

½ teaspoon salt

1½ cups canola or other neutral vegetable oil, or ¾ cup canola and ¾ cup olive oil

Crack the egg into the bowl of a blender or food processor and add the mustard, lemon juice, and salt. Blend on low speed until completely smooth. With the motor running, slowly pour in the oil, at first only a few drops at a time, then in a thin stream as the mixture begins to thicken, until all the oil is incorporated; at this point, you've got mayo. Transfer to an airtight container and refrigerate for up to 2 weeks.

WHOLE WHEAT PIZZA DOUGH

MAKES 1 (13-INCH) CRUST

1 tablespoon honey

¾ cup warm water

1 packet (2¼ teaspoons) instant yeast

¼ cup whole milk yogurt

2 cups whole wheat flour

2 teaspoons salt

2 tablespoons extra-virgin olive oil

For those of you filled with fear and trepidation at the thought of making yeasted dough, I encourage you to let go of your doubts. My recipe is as quick, simple, and fail-proof as can be, owing to the fact that I call for instant yeast, which is fast acting and doesn't require proofing. (SAF Red Instant Yeast is my preferred brand.) It's also healthy and flavor-packed, thanks to the whole wheat and yogurt, a real upgrade from supermarket versions. And the dough takes only about 30 minutes to whip together, so you can easily make it and gather your pizza fixings while the dough is resting—or make it ahead of time and pull it out of the fridge for an impromptu pizza party.

In a medium mixing bowl, stir together the honey and water and then sprinkle the yeast evenly over the top. Add the yogurt, flour, salt, and olive oil and stir with a wooden spoon or rubber spatula until the flour is completely incorporated. The dough should be soft and somewhat sticky but hold its shape. Cover the bowl with plastic wrap and let the dough rest for 10 minutes.

Uncover the dough, dust it lightly with additional flour, and knead it in the bowl for about 1 minute, until it becomes resilient and springs back, dusting with additional flour as needed to prevent it from sticking to your hands. At this point the dough will be able to hold a round shape, but the surface won't be completely smooth. Recover the bowl tightly with plastic wrap and set aside at room temperature.

If you're planning on using the dough to make pizza the same day, let the dough rise for 30 minutes. Depending on how warm the ambient temperature is, the dough may rise only slightly, or not at all. (Don't worry, the yeast will do its work in the oven—and pizza is, after all, a flatbread.)

Alternatively, if you're making the dough in advance, make sure the bowl is tightly sealed in plastic wrap and refrigerate for up to 3 days. When you're ready to use the dough and make a pizza, preheat the oven to 450°F. Remove the dough from the refrigerator, roll it out on a floured countertop, and transfer to a greased baking sheet lined with parchment paper (see Mushroom and Goat Cheese Pizza, page 155, for details). There's no need to let it come to room temperature; in fact, it's easier to roll if slightly cool. Add your favorite toppings and bake for approximately 25 to 30 minutes, until the edges of the crust and cheese are deep golden brown and crisped.

FLAKY BUTTERMILK BISCUITS

Popping open a can of dough is as close as many Americans get to making biscuits from scratch. Store-bought biscuit dough certainly offers convenience, but if you have a little extra time on your hands, you won't regret making my buttery, flaky homemade version. It undoubtably will elevate your fried chicken sandwich (see page 44). I'm not one to eschew convenience entirely, however—I call for self-rising flour because it means you don't have to measure out separate leavening ingredients.

Preheat the oven to 425°F. Line a baking sheet with parchment paper and set aside.

In a medium mixing bowl, whisk together the flour, sugar, and salt to combine. Toss in the butter and, using your fingers or a pastry cutter, work in the butter until the mixture is sandy, with the largest pieces of butter being no larger than the size of a pea. Add ½ cup of the buttermilk and, using a rubber spatula or wooden spoon, mix until just combined and the dough holds together. (Add additional buttermilk, 1 tablespoon at a time, to moisten the flour if it's too dry.) Shape the dough into a flat square about 1 inch thick, wrap with plastic wrap, and chill for at least 30 minutes or up to 1 hour.

Transfer the dough to a lightly floured surface and roll into a ¼-inch-thick, approximately 14 by 8-inch rectangle. Take the two shorter sides and fold them so that their edges meet together in the center, then fold in half again along the seam formed by the first fold (like closing a book), forming four layers.

Dusting with more flour as needed to prevent sticking, roll the newly formed rectangle into a ½-inch-thick, approximately 10 by 6-inch rectangle. Cut the dough into eight squares approximately 2½ inches per side (or use a ring cutter). Transfer the biscuits onto the prepared baking sheet, leaving at least 2 inches between each.

Bake for 20 to 25 minutes, rotating the pan halfway through, until the biscuits are puffed and golden brown (lowering heat as necessary to prevent overbrowning).

MAKES ABOUT 8 BISCUITS

2½ cups self-rising flour

1 tablespoon sugar

1 teaspoon salt

12 tablespoons unsalted butter, cold, cut into ½-inch dice

½ to 1 cup buttermilk or kefir (often sold as drinking yogurt)

ALL-PURPOSE STOCK

3 to 4 pounds assorted meaty bone pieces and or meat scraps (such as veal, pork, poultry, beef, or a mixture of the four)

6 quarts cold water

1 large white or yellow onion, peeled and halved through root end

2 carrots, cut into 3-inch pieces

2 celery stalks, cut into 3-inch pieces

1 small head garlic, halved crosswise

3 parsley stems (reserve leaves for another use)

3 sprigs of thyme

½ teaspoon white or black peppercorns, or a mixture

1 bay leaf

Making your own stock certainly isn't required for making the delicious soups, stews, and other spin-off dishes in this book. But this dead-simple, stove-top version that simmers away on your back burner while you're doing other things will give you results that are vastly superior to anything that comes from a can or a box.

Think of this recipe as a blueprint, rather than something you have to follow slavishly. You can make it using any type of leftover bones and meat scraps that can be stored in the freezer until you've accumulated enough to make a batch. I recommend using portions of bone with meat still attached and with plenty of connective tissue, which will impart gelatin, add body, and produce a richer, more flavorful stock.

Place the bones and meat scraps in a colander and rinse under cold running water for 1 to 2 minutes, to wash away any blood or impurities.

Transfer the bones and scraps to a large (2-gallon) stockpot, along with the water, and bring to a boil over medium-high heat. Reduce the heat to a simmer and, using a slotted spoon or ladle, skim away any scum that floats to the surface. Continue to simmer for 30 minutes, skimming away any fat that rises to the surface. Add the onion, carrot, celery, and garlic and simmer for at least 2 hours, or up to 6 hours, until the broth has taken on a rich golden color and the bones have begun to soften and fall apart. Add the parsley, thyme, peppercorns, and bay leaf and simmer for 30 minutes more. Remove from the heat.

Strain the stock through a fine sieve (or a colander lined with cheesecloth) into a large bowl and discard the solids. If desired, skim off any remaining fat that floats to the top with a spoon or ladle.

Allow the stock to cool completely and then transfer to a large, airtight container, two 1-gallon ziplock bags, or ice cube trays (perfect for smaller portions), or a combination, which will widen your options to use the stock later on. Once chilled, the stock can be stored in the refrigerator for up to 1 week or in the freezer for up to 2 months.

To return frozen stock to its liquid state, it can be thawed overnight in the fridge, heated in the microwave or on the stove top, or warmed up in a water bath at 55°C (131°F) or above for 30 minutes.

BEYOND THE RECIPES

The recipes in this book show how sous vide can minimize your time in the kitchen to get dinner on the table in under an hour. Still, I understand that many people are looking for a cooking solution that requires the shortest cooking time and fewest number of pots and pans as possible, so there's an even simpler approach you can take. I call them one-bag meals.

ONE-BAG MEALS

This "bath-to-plate" method calls for adding your favorite sauce, marinade, or spice rub directly in the sous vide bag along with whatever you're cooking. When combined with the flavorful cooking juices that collect in the bag, the sauce becomes the basis for a ready-to-eat meal, so all you need to do is open the bag, pour or ladle the contents into your bowl, and dinner is served. While this approach doesn't give you the opportunity to build additional flavor or achieve that coveted crust that occurs only during searing, the trade-off is a dead-simple meal with minimal prep or cleanup time.

Keep in mind, there are some rules of thumb when making a one-bag meal:

» Choose tender and quick-cooking proteins such as boneless, skinless chicken and seafood (like peeled shrimp or skinless salmon); lean cuts of pork and beef. Cut into bite-size pieces so they cook quickly.

» Season your food with salt before cooking, but reduce the amount if your sauce or rub contains a lot of salt. If you want to add herbs and spices to the bag (page 10), use a smaller amount than you would typically. Note that woody herbs (such as thyme and rosemary) and raw garlic can be become bitter or overbearing when cooked sous vide at low temperatures.

» Add sauce directly into the bag and toss well to coat the food evenly. For every 1 pound of protein, use approximately 1 cup of sauce, ⅛ to ¼ cup of marinade, or 1 or 2 tablespoons of spice rub. There's no magic number here—you're just looking to add enough to season the food and end up with enough liquid for a finishing sauce. The cooking liquid from your protein or vegetables will thin out the sauce slightly.

» Make sure that your food is arranged in a single, even layer in the bag, rather than sitting in a clump at the bottom, to ensure even cooking.

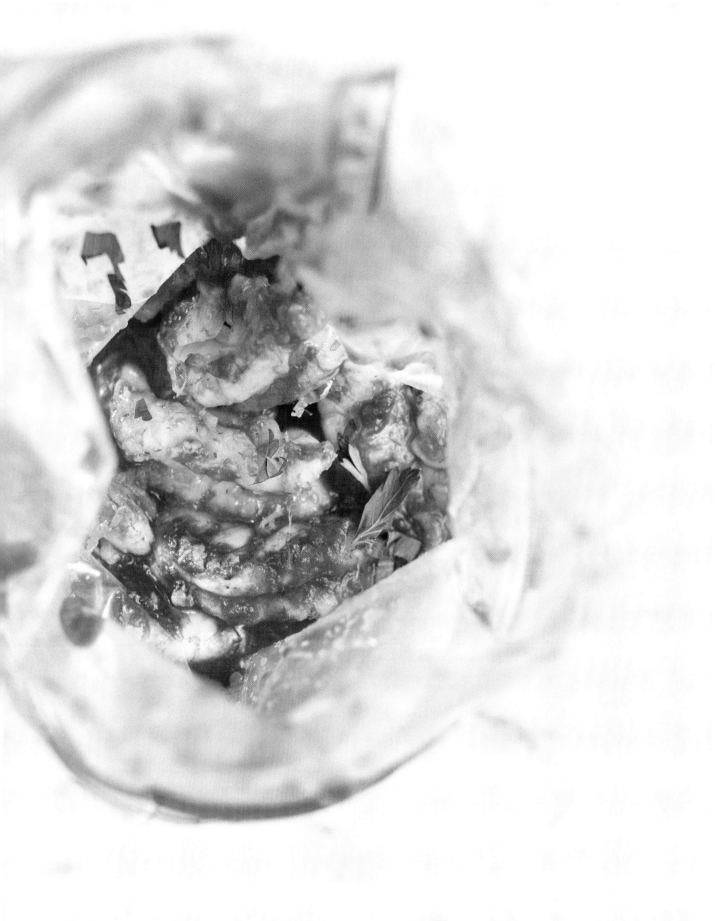

If you can't fit all the pieces in one bag easily, divide them into two bags (a 1-gallon bag holds about 3 pounds of protein).

» Seal your bag according to the best method. If adding a liquid such as marinade or sauce, seal using the table-edge method (page 13). The water displacement method (page 12) is fine for dry rubs.

» Once you've sealed your bag, lay it on a flat surface and flatten the contents with your hands to even out the thickness. If you notice the pieces bunching up during the cooking process, pull out the bag, massage the contents (covering it with a dish towel if the bag is too hot to handle), and reflatten. (For anything cooked for longer than 3 hours, there's no need to keep a close eye because at that point you can be confident that the food will be heated through.)

» Refer to the cooking chart on page 182 or the corresponding master recipe in this book to determine the proper cooking temperature for your ingredients. Increase the minimum cooking time by 50 percent to account for the added weight of the marinade or sauce.

You can also apply this one-bag meal approach to any master recipe in this book after it's been cooked. Simply cook an unadorned piece of protein or vegetable according to the master recipe instructions, remove from the bag, and sear for a few minutes on both sides (to build flavor). Then return it to the bag, add some sauce, reseal, and heat in the water bath for another 10 minutes to warm through before serving.

Likewise, if you want to stockpile some ready-to-eat meals for later in the week, open the bag of cooked food, add a finished sauce, chill in an ice water bath (see page 18), and store in the fridge for up to 1 week. Then simply reheat at the same temperature at which you cooked it (see reheating, page 18).

Here are some simple but delicious one-bag meals you might consider:

» Shrimp in spicy marinara sauce (homemade, page 47, or store-bought) for a fast Fra Diavolo

» Pork loin in salsa verde (homemade, page 73, or store-bought) for a simple Colorado green chili

» Salmon in teriyaki marinade for an easy Japanese meal

» Chicken breasts in barbecue sauce for indoor BBQ night

» Cauliflower in curry sauce for an easy tikka masala

» Chicken thighs in adobo sauce for a low-stress Mexican feast

HOW TO ADAPT ANY RECIPE TO SOUS VIDE

If there's a single message I want this book to drive home, it's that sous vide is a wonderful technique for *everyone*, from amateurs to master chefs, diet fanatics to gluttons (here's where I raise my hand). Furthermore, sous vide is also beholden to no one cuisine or set of flavors—it's simply a technique that gives you precision and control to produce exactly the results you want. Of course I hope you love the recipes I've gathered in this book as much as my family and I do, but my greatest hope is that you learn to make sous vide your own.

I want you to feel free to not only adapt my recipes to your own tastes, but also to take recipes that you already love and see how this technique can make them easier and maybe even better. I know, it might sound like blasphemy to say that this newfangled contraption can improve a treasured family recipe. But keep in mind that at some point *all* cooking tools were new—and cooking is not only about preserving tradition, it's also about changing traditions to fit into modern life.

To give you an idea of what adapting a recipe using traditional cooking methods to sous vide looks like, let's say that you have a beloved recipe for Southern smothered pork chops, but you want to take the dish to the next level using sous vide to ensure perfectly cooked rosy pork. The recipe likely will have you sear the chops, set them aside, then build a sauce in the pan before "smothering" the pork in the sauce and simmering it to finish the cooking. To adapt the recipe following the formula I use in this book, I would use the master recipe for pork loin cuts (58°C for 1 hour, in this case) to cook the pork chops sous vide. Once cooked, the chops are ready to be used in the recipe, or they can be chilled and refrigerated to be finished another time. To finish your sous vide version of this dish, season and sear the pork as you would normally, continuing through the sauce-making step—but now there's no need for the final cooking step. By going the sous vide route, you've improved the dish by guaranteeing that your pork is perfectly cooked, and, if you prepped the pork ahead of time, you've also substantially cut down on the time it takes to get your food to the table at dinnertime. It's sous vide magic!

I encourage you to use this same approach to enhance any cherished recipe in your repertoire, or those culled from your favorite magazine or blog. Simply reference the relevant master recipe (or use the handy chart on page 182) to find the appropriate time and temperature for the recipe you want to make. If you already have a cooked master recipe on hand, you can even use this method to sous-vidify a dish you've never made before. That's what this book is all about: sous vide giving you the confidence to improvise freely and cook like a pro.

Flank Steak.
Burritos   -Donna
From the kitchen of Ronda's HOT CHICKEN

Flank Steak.
...bread crumbs.
...salt...pepper.
...Chopped celery.
...onion chopped.
...butter or margarine...add other...
...celery in butter, roll out...
...break in meat...fill pocket...

Carrot -
1 C. nuts chopped
1 c. salad oil
3 eggs
1/3 c. water
1½ c. sugar
1½ c. flour
½ t. nutmeg
1 t. cinnamon
1 t. soda
1 t. salt
3 medium sized carrots

Mix all ingredients...
until smooth. Pour in...
Bake at 350° for 30 or...
Ice with butter icing:
3/4 package...
1 cube butter
vanilla and...
thick icing.

Burritos   -Donna
...large flour tortillas (Ralph...
...beef (a lb.
...large can refried beans
...seasonings to taste : chili powder...
...string cheese (Cracker Bar...
...meat mixture in center of...
...top with chee...

From the kitchen of...
Beef Stroganauf - serves 5-6
1½# beef top round - cut in strips
½ c. butter
1 onion   ½ c. sour cream
3/4# sliced mushrooms   ½ - 3/4 c. heavy cream
3 T flour   4 cups rice
1½ c. beef bullion
3/4 t salt
3 T tomato sauce
1 t worchershire sauce
FL Madere - 11/63

Rice consomme in green peppers
Rice: use Minute Rice
1 cube margerine
1 onion diced
2 cans beef consomme - add...
   to total...
   quant...
Oven: 30
Parboil gr...

Just to let you know
"what's cookin"
Virginia Hatcher - '66
Crab Supreme
8 slices bread
2 cup crab meat
1 yellow onion, chopped
½ cup mayonnaise
1 c. celery chopped
...can mushroom...
...cheese

From the kitchen of Ronda's HOT CHICKEN
4 cups chicken or Turkey
1 T minced onion
2 c chopped celery
2 T lemon juice
3/4 c mayonnaise
1 can cr of chicken soup
1 tsp salt
4 hardboiled eggs (cut up)
Combine ingredients...
place in buttered 9 X 13" pan...
anita beck

4 eggs
dressing mix - 1 pack
parmesan cheese
Mozarello cheese - 1 ball
2 cans tomato sauce
salt + pepper to taste
Beat 4 eggs with salt + pepper
veal. Pulverize dressing, add...

...(1½ cups) chicken...
...strips
...(lb.) diced or raw American cheese
...milk

Fancy Chicken Casserole Serves 4-5 4 cook...
from the kitchen of Faith Rhodes
Blend together 1 can c/ of
mushroom + 1 can c/ of
chicken. Fold in 1⅓...
...not
...well
...pan.
...chicken
...in...

Pudding Sauce (Mother) - 19
⅓ C sugar   1 T margarin...
1 T flour   3 mix dry   creamed w...
pinch salt   dry ingre...
Add 1 cup boiling water...
smooth, bring to boil. Add fla...
as desired (vanilla, lemon, alm...
nutmeg, etc.)

RIB ROAST OF
Season standing rib roast with salt and...
in shallow baking pan, fat side up. R...
slow oven (325°F.) to desired degree...
halves in roasting pan with roast the...
cooking time. Garnish platter with pea...

Rare beef:	5 to 6 lb. ro...
	7 to 8 lb. ro...
Medium beef:	5 to 6 lb. roast —...
	7 to 8 lb. ro...
Well done beef:	5 to 6 lb. roast —...
	7 to 8 lb. roast — 25...

This guide is for chilled beef, which has been...

GLAND

Fancy Chicken Cass...
Blend together 1 can c/of
mushroom + 1 can c/of
chicken soup. Fol...
cups Minute Rice (raw)
in well buttered baki...
pan. Lay pieces of ra...
chicken (about half a...
with 1 pkg. dry onion...

Elisa Bagdasar 7/74
Cabbage R...
1 head cabbage -...
Core & break leaves...
boiling water for 4-5...
Meat Mixture
1½ lb. ground beef or lamb...
combination
½ c. rice - regular (Minute Braw
1/4 c. bulgar (cracked wheat or
...ralston or wheat Heart...
...Raston or wheat Heart)...
...instructions for...
very simple.
For eight to ten...
about 3 lbs shrimp...
cleaned ; mix with...

Filet of Sole Fromage
1 lb white fish
1 can cheddar soup undilut...
½ t lemon juice
sprinkling of dill seed - 1 T
blend + pour over
fish rolled + toothpick...
Bake 40 min. at 350°

Here's What's Cookin'
Recipe from the Kitchen of...
Serves
3 lbs top steak
Meat
1 can cream of mush...
room soup
1 can onion soup
1 cup burgundy
wine
1 can mushrooms
(piece)
1/2 cup -
(drain fat after...
is gone)
Add:

(Hilda Rohr...

TIME AND TEMPERATURE COOKING GUIDE

Should you want to venture out further than the recipes in this book, I've created this time and temperature cooking guide. However, it doesn't include every possible permutation. For instance, I've given you directions for boneless *and* bone-in chicken thighs because they are easy to find in stores, but only bone-in duck legs because boneless duck thighs are not common. If there's something you don't see on this chart, I encourage you to go to the Library of Google, which will help you find instructions on preparing more obscure victuals like kangaroo or alligator.*

Note that all measurements indicated here are measured at the food's thickest point, and for each one, I went with what I considered to be the average size for that particular item. Naturally, sizes vary, so to figure out the proper cooking time for larger cuts, follow this rule of thumb: For poultry, meat, and vegetables, increase the cooking time by 1 hour for every additional 1 inch of thickness. For seafood, on the other hand, increase the cooking time by 15 minutes for every 1 inch of thickness.

EGGS (ALL SIZES)

"Raw" pasteurizing	57°C (134.6°F)	2 to 4 hours
Whites opaque, yolk runny and unable to hold shape	60°C (140°F)	1 to 2 hours
Whites delicate but hold shape, yolk liquid but slightly thickened	62°C to 63°C (143.6°F-145.4°F)	1 to 2 hours
Whites delicate but hold shape, yolk fudgy and spreadable	64°C (147.2°F)	1 to 2 hours
Soft boiled	85°C (185°F)	12 minutes
Hard boiled	85°C (185°F)	25 to 30 minutes

POULTRY

Chicken breast, boneless, about 1½ inches thick	63°C (145.4°F)	1 to 5 hours
Chicken breast, bone-in, about 2½ inches thick	63°C (145.4°F)	2 to 6 hours
Chicken thigh, boneless, about 1 inch thick	65°C (149°)	1½ to 6 hours
Chicken thigh, bone-in, about 2 inches thick	70°C (158°F)	2 to 7 hours
Turkey breast, boneless, about 4 inches thick	62°C (143.6°F)	4 to 8 hours
Turkey thighs and legs, bone-in, about 4 inches thick	68°C (154.4°F)	6 to 12 hours
Duck breast, boneless, about 1½ inches thick	55°C (131°F)	1 to 5 hours
Duck thighs, bone-in, about 2½ inches thick	80°C (175°F)	8 to 12 hours
Spatchcocked whole small game birds (quail), about 1½ inch thick	60°C (140°F)	1 to 5 hours
Larger game birds (pheasant, guinea hen), broken down into quarters/bone-in breast and leg pieces, about 2½ inches thick	60°C (140°F)	2 to 5 hours

PORK AND VEAL

Loin cuts (tenderloin and chops), boneless or bone-in, about 1 ½ inch thick	58°C (136.4°F)	1½ to 5 hours
Tougher cuts (belly, breast, shoulder, ribs), boneless or bone-in, 2 to 4 inches thick	75°C (167°F)	15 to 20 hours

SAUSAGES AND MEATBALLS

Meat or poultry, about 1½ inches thick	65°C (149°)	1½ to 5 hours

BEEF

Steak loin cuts (NY strip, rib eye, tenderloin), bone-in or boneless, about 1½ inches thick		
Rare	50°C (122°F)	1 to 2 hours
Medium rare	55°C (131°F)	1 to 5 hours
Medium	60°C (140°F)	1 to 5 hours
Tougher steak cuts (Skirt, flank, hanger, tri-tip), boneless, about 1 inch thick		
Rare	50°C (122°F)	1 to 2 hours
Medium rare	55°C (131°F)	1 to 12 hours
Medium	60°C (140°F)	1 to 12 hours
Chuck and sirloin cuts for braising (flatiron, bavette, coulotte), boneless, about 1½ inches thick	65°C (149°)	18 to 30 hours
Tougher cuts for braising (brisket, short ribs, oxtail, shank), bone-in or boneless	70°C (158°F)	18 to 36 hours

LAMB AND VENISON

Rack, about 2½ inches thick	55°C (131°F)	2 to 5 hours
Loin, about 2 inches thick	55°C (131°F)	1½ to 4 hours
Leg or shoulder, boneless, about 4 inches thick	68°C (154.4°F)	8 to 16 hours

RABBIT

Legs, bone-in, about 1½ inch thick	65°C (149°)	1½ to 5 hours
Saddle/loin, bone-in, about 2½ inches thick	60°C (140°F)	2 to 5 hours
Saddle/loin boneless, about 1 inch thick	60°C (140°F)	1 to 5 hours

SHRIMP

Large (16/20) shrimp, 16 to 20 per pound, about ¾ inch thick	60°C (140°F)	15 to 25 minutes

LOBSTER

Tails, whole, about 2 inches thick	60°C (140°F)	30 to 60 minutes

OCTOPUS

Whole, about 3 pounds	84°C (183.2°F)	4 to 6 hours

FLAKY WHITE FISH (HALIBUT, TROUT, COD, SEA BASS, ETC.)

Fillets, whole or cut into pieces, about 1 to 1½ inches thick		
Medium cooked (firmer and almost fully opaque)	55°C (131°F)	20 to 30 minutes
Fully cooked (firm and fully opaque)	60°C (140°F)	20 to 30 minutes

SALMON

Boneless fillet pieces, 1 to 1½ inches thick		
Lightly cooked (very delicate and just barely opaque)	52.5°C (126.5°F)	20 to 30 minutes
Medium cooked (firmer and almost fully opaque)	55°C (131°F)	20 to 30 minutes
Fully cooked (firm and fully opaque)	60°C (140°F)	20 to 30 minutes

STARCHY VEGETABLES (POTATOES, CARROTS, SQUASH, BEETS, SWEET POTATOES, TURNIPS, ETC.)

Pieces cut to about 1 inch thick	85°C (185°F)	1 to 2 hours

CAULIFLOWER

Pieces cut to about 1 inch thick	85°C (185°F)	25 to 60 minutes

MUSHROOMS (ALL VARIETIES)

Whole or pieces, no more than 1 inch thick	85°C (185°F)	15 to 30 minutes

LIQUOR INFUSIONS

In a bag, about 2 to 4 cups (½ to 1 liter)	60°C (140°F)	1 to 2 hours
In a jar or bottle, about 2 to 4 cups (½ to 1 liter)	60°C (140°F)	2 to 3 hours

CUSTARD

"Baked-style" custard in 4-ounce jars (such as pot de crème, crème brulee)	80°C (176.4°F)	75 to 120 minutes (see note on tempering glass on page 20)
Poured custard, about 1 to 2 quarts (such as ice cream base, lemon curd)	83°C (181.4°F)	60 to 90 minutes

* Although you can find sous vide recipes for everyday items such as grains, dried legumes, and green vegetables, I've intentionally left them off this chart. After much experimentation, I've come to the conclusion that using sous vide for those items is more trouble than it's worth, so I recommend cooking them conventionally.

MEASUREMENT CONVERSION CHARTS

LENGTH

Inch	Metric
¼ inch	6 mm
½ inch	1.25 cm
¾ inch	2 cm
1 inch	2.5 cm
6 inches (½ foot)	15 cm
12 inches (1 foot)	30 cm

VOLUME

US	Imperial	Metric
1 tablespoon	½ fl oz	15 ml
2 tablespoons	1 fl oz	30 ml
¼ cup	2 fl oz	60 ml
⅓ cup	3 fl oz	90 ml
½ cup	4 fl oz	120 ml
⅔ cup	5 fl oz (¼ pint)	150 ml
¾ cup	6 fl oz	180 ml
1 cup	8 fl oz (⅓ pint)	240 ml
1¼ cups	10 fl oz (½ pint)	300 ml
2 cups (1 pint)	16 fl oz (⅔ pint)	480 ml
2½ cups	20 fl oz (1 pint)	600 ml
1 quart	32 fl oz (1⅔ pints)	1 l

WEIGHT

US/Imperial	Metric
½ oz	15 g
1 oz	30 g
2 oz	60 g
¼ lb	115 g
⅓ lb	150 g
½ lb	225 g
¾ lb	350 g
1 lb	450 g

ABOUT THE AUTHORS

LISA Q. FETTERMAN

is the founder and CEO of Nomiku, makers of the first home immersion circulator. She has been featured in *Wired*, *MAKE*, and *Forbes*, and was named on *Forbes'*, *Inc.* magazine, and Zagat Survey's 30 Under 30 lists for her pioneering work in the food space. Lisa earned a BA in journalism from NYU and honed her culinary sensibilities working at some of the top restaurants in the country, including Babbo, Jean-Georges, and Saison. She lives in San Francisco with her husband and Nomiku cofounder. Together they've launched the Nomiku Meals experience, which ships delicious, ready-to-eat sous vide meals directly to your door.

MEESHA HALM

is a content strategist, cookbook whisperer, and digital storyteller. She is the author of over 20 restaurant guides and cookbooks including *The Balsamic Vinegar Cookbook*, and *Savoring the Wine Country*. She served as a local editor for Zagat Survey, video producer for Tastemade, and cookbook editor at Collins. Her writing and videos have appeared on The Food Network, Tasting Table, Zagat, Michelin, Bravo, and Tastemade.

SCOTT PEABODY

is a professional chef with more than a decade and a half of experience. He attended the Culinary Institute of America in Hyde Park before cutting his teeth in New York City, toiling in the kitchens of renowned chefs Jean-Georges Vongerichten and Thomas Keller, where he was initiated into the mysteries of sous vide cooking. Scott provided the recipes and culinary direction for this book.

MONICA LO

is a creative director and photographer for various brands in the food and cannabis space. Monica is the creator of Sous Weed and a photo contributor for Stock Pot Images and Menu Stories. Monica has been featured on the TODAY Show, MSNBC, Huffington Post, and VICE Munchies for her work. Monica provided the photography for this book.

Together they are also the authors and photographer of *Sous Vide at Home*.

Photos by Rebecca Simonne Goberstein

ACKNOWLEDGMENTS

The entire creative team is truly grateful to the many, many people who helped make this cookbook a reality. In particular, we would like to thank:

Jenny Wapner and the rest of the team at Ten Speed Press, for supporting our last book and giving us the opportunity to do it all over again.

Sally Ekus, our literary agent for this cookbook, for her unwavering support and enthusiasm for this project.

Monica Lo, for bringing life to all the beautiful, mouth-watering pictures in this book.

Virgina Willis, our seasoned recipe tester, for lending her experience and sharp eye for detail.

Danielle Wallis, prop stylist par excellence, for schlepping up from LA to make our photo shoot a dream.

Leigh Saffold, for her keen editorial guidance that helped bring this book to completion.

Christine Wolheim, for styling a cover-worthy shot.

Mar Mar Keenan of MMclay and Jenny Dorsey of Wednesday Ceramics, both of whose beautiful pieces appear in this book.

June Lee, who provided both props and advice on Korean cooking.

To everyone who provided their treasured vintage recipe cards: Hilda Rohr (whose impeccable handwriting inspired the idea), Rondi Dralle, Robin Peabody, and Diana Haven, who shared her great-great mother Mabel Hodgkinson's cherished recipe box with us.

FROM LISA

First and foremost, I owe my deepest gratitude to my collaborators: Meesha, whose patience and dedication steered this ship successfully to safe harbor, and Scott, whose vision and passion run through every recipe in this book. Your hard work made it all possible—thanks for making magic yet again!

Team Members of Nomiku past and present, for spreading the gospel of sous vide globally!

Jim Eber, for giving me the best advice, both professionally and personally.

Last but not least, my heartfelt thanks to my wonderful family. Abe, my husband and co-founder, for being my rock. My father Charles Qiu, my mother Tina Wang, and my mother-in-law Deborah Lloyd, for helping raise my beautiful children, Zechariah and Margeaux, and keeping our lives together while we were in the trenches.

FROM MEESHA

Eternal gratitude to my supportive husband Jon Fox and wonderful teenagers Olive and Jude, for their enduring love and support, and for putting up with the endless humming of sous vide machines, involuntary recipe-testing dinners, and marathon writing sessions at the dining room table that relegated them to another room. And to my late mother Beverly Halm, who instilled in me my love of cooking and taught me the real meaning of the B.C.

FROM SCOTT

My profound and abiding thanks to the wonderful friends and family whose advice and support helped me navigate this arduous process once more—but especially to my mother, Robin, who knows a thing or two about what it takes to get a meal on the table and the value of sharing food.

INDEX

Library of Congress Cataloging-in-Publication Data
  Names: Fetterman, Lisa Q., author. | Halm, Meesha, author. | Peabody, Scott,
    author. | Lo, Monica, photographer.
Title: Sous vide made simple : 60 everyday recipes for perfectly cooked meals
  / Lisa Q. Fetterman, Meesha Halm, and Scott Peabody ; and photographs by
  Monica Lo.
Description: First edition. | New York : Ten Speed Press, an imprint of the
  Crown Publishing Group, a division of Penguin Random House LLC, [2018] |
Includes index.
Identifiers: LCCN 2018025089
Subjects: LCSH: Sous-vide cooking. | LCGFT: Cookbooks.
Classification: LCC TX690.7 .F483 2018 | DDC 641.5/87—dc23
LC record available at https://lccn.loc.gov/2018025089

Hardcover ISBN: ISBN 978-0-399-58201-1
ebook ISBN 978-0-399-58202-8

Printed in United States of America

Design by Annie Marino
Interior food styling by Scott Peabody
Interior prop styling by Danielle Wallis
Food and prop styling on the cover, page 46, and page 49 by Christine Wolheim

10 9 8 7 6 5 4 3 2 1

First Edition